GACE

Special Education General Curriculum Practice Questions

Mometrix

TEST PREPARATION

Dear Future Exam Success Story

First of all, **THANK YOU** for purchasing Mometrix study materials!

Second, congratulations! You are one of the few determined test-takers who are committed to doing whatever it takes to excel on your exam. **You have come to the right place.** We developed these practice tests with one goal in mind: to deliver you the best possible approximation of the questions you will see on test day.

Standardized testing is one of the biggest obstacles on your road to success, which only increases the importance of doing well in the high-pressure, high-stakes environment of test day. Your results on this test could have a significant impact on your future, and these practice tests will give you the repetitions you need to build your familiarity and confidence with the test content and format to help you achieve your full potential on test day.

Your success is our success

We would love to hear from you! If you would like to share the story of your exam success or if you have any questions or comments in regard to our products, please contact us at **800-673-8175** or **support@mometrix.com**.

Thanks again for your business and we wish you continued success!

Sincerely,
The Mometrix Test Preparation Team

Printed in the United States of America

TABLE OF CONTENTS

Practice Test #1

1. An intellectually disabled teen has been offered a job by an elderly neighbor. The neighbor wants the teen to work alongside her in the garden twice a week. They will plant seeds, transplant larger plants, weed, lay mulch, water and fertilize. Later in the season, they will cut flowers and arrange bouquets, pick produce and sell them at the neighbor's roadside stand. The neighbor, the teen's mother and special education teacher meet to discuss the proposal. The plan is:

a. Tentatively accepted. Because the teen is excited about having a job, her mother and teacher reluctantly agree. They both know the girl is likely to lose interest quickly and caution the neighbor that if she truly needs help she may want to look elsewhere. However, no one wants to disappoint the girl and all decide the experience will be good for her.
b. Rejected. Despite the teen's insistence she can manage these tasks, her mother and teacher believe she cannot. They fear trying will set her up for failure.
c. Rejected. The teacher and her mother are very uncomfortable with the neighbor's offer. They suspect the elderly woman is simply lonely or may be a predator who has selected an intellectually disabled victim because such children are particularly vulnerable.
d. Enthusiastically accepted. The adults discuss a background check and the possibility the teen might discover gardening is not for her and want to quit. However, this is most likely to happen early in her employment, giving the neighbor sufficient time to find another helper.

2. Which of the following issues would be most likely to arise when teaching a large group of students with a wide range of disabilities?

a. The teacher may not be able to meet the student's IEP goals.
b. The teacher may not be able to provide accommodations.
c. The teacher may not be able to incorporate assistive technology.
d. The teacher may not be able to appropriately differentiate.

3. Which one of the following federal laws currently governs special education services in the United States?

a. Section 504 of the Rehabilitation Act
b. Individuals with Disabilities Education Act
c. Family Educational Rights and Privacy Act
d. Americans with Disabilities Act

4. Which of the following assistive technologies is most indicated for a student who has difficulties with memory retrieval?

a. Voice recognition software
b. Word prediction software
c. Speech output software
d. Spell checker software

5. Which of the following strategies can a special education teacher implement to best ensure that inclusion is successful in their school?

a. Articulating the need for inclusion to the school administrators
b. Collaborating with general education teachers
c. Developing new assessments to measure student growth
d. Providing professional development to staff

6. A teacher suspects one of her kindergarteners has a learning disability in math. Why would the teacher suggest intervention to the child's concerned parents rather than assessment as the first step?

a. She wouldn't; assessment should precede intervention
b. She wouldn't; kindergarteners develop new skills at radically different rates. Suggesting either intervention or assessment at this point is premature. The teacher would more likely observe the child over a three month period to note her development before including the parents about her concern
c. Assessing a young child for learning disabilities often leads to an incorrect conclusion because a student must be taught the subject before it's possible to assess her understanding of it. Intervention teaches the child specific skills to correct her misconceptions. If the intervention fails, assessment is the next step
d. Assessment at this stage is unnecessary and wastes time and money. Since an assessment that resulted in a diagnosis of a learning disability would recommend intervention to correct it, it is more efficient to proceed directly to intervention

7. Which of the following statements is most true about adaptations teachers may need to use in testing, teaching, and materials to address the needs of individual students?

a. Some students use communication modes unfamiliar to the teacher
b. Differentiation of instruction is unnecessary between boys and girls
c. Teachers are unlikely to encounter age differences in the same class
d. Students speaking other languages must quickly adapt to using English

8. Which of the following is NOT primarily an assessment of adaptive skills?

a. The Walker-McConnell
b. The Vineland
c. The WISC-IV
d. The SSRS

9. Richard is a sophomore in high school who is nonverbal. Which assistive technology devices would be MOST beneficial in allowing him to communicate effectively?

a. Audio players
b. FM listening systems
c. Schedule boards
d. Graphic organizers

10. What is not a characteristic of a writing disorder?

a. Poor organizational skills
b. Weak phonological skills
c. Inadequate vocabulary
d. Weak planning abilities

11. One of the most important assessment tools for students with specific learning disabilities is a curriculum-based measure. Which of the following describes the MOST effective use of this kind of measure?

a. To determine whether or not a student is keeping up with his or her peers
b. To determine whether or not a student is making progress on his or her Individualized Education Program (IEP) goals
c. To determine whether or not a student is learning the curriculum
d. To determine whether or not a student has mastery of the curriculum

12. Which one of the following strategies is most beneficial in maintaining a safe learning environment?

a. Teaching at the front of the classroom
b. Walking around the classroom while teaching
c. A combination of teaching at the front and walking around
d. Sitting with the students while teaching

13. Approximately what percentage of the population is classified as intellectually disabled?

a. Less than 1%
b. 1 to 2%
c. 2 to 3%
d. 3 to 4%

14. Which of the following is true of co-occurring conditions for students with ADHD who receive special education services?

a. Anxiety is the most common co-occurring disorder for students with ADHD.
b. Speech problems are more common in students without ADHD.
c. Almost half of students with ADHD also have a learning disability.
d. The majority of students with ADHD have conduct disorders.

15. The desired outcomes a teacher places on his or her students can also be referred to as what?

a. Goals
b. Expectations
c. Rules
d. Procedures

16. According to the Individuals with Disabilities Education Act (IDEA), which condition could fall under the umbrella term of *specific learning disability*?

a. Speech or language impairment
b. Auditory processing disorder
c. Attention deficit disorder
d. Bipolar disorder

17. Mr. John and Ms. Deere are team-teaching a special education class of high school students who are deaf or hard of hearing. Mr. John has written a lesson plan of multimodal activities based around a scenario involving a boys' basketball team. Ms. Deere is recommending some changes to this lesson plan as she feels it is biased. Which of the following is the most likely basis for her objections?

a. Mr. John's lesson plan is not likely to be one to which the female students can relate.
b. Mr. John's lesson plan is not likely to appeal to students with hearing impairments.
c. Mr. John's lesson plan did not include any input from Ms. Deere when he wrote it.
d. Mr. John's lesson plan focuses on a physical education activity with no academics.

18. Students with learning disabilities will typically spend part or all of their day in what type of classroom?

a. General classroom
b. Solitary classroom
c. Special education classroom
d. Language learning classroom

19. Andrea is a first-grade student with a developmental delay. How can a formative assessment be implemented to monitor her progress throughout the school year?

a. Interviewing her each week
b. Giving her academic probes
c. Observing her in class
d. Monitoring her test scores

20. When conducting an assessment in the area of fine motor skills, which of the following activities would be the most important to observe?

a. Watching a student draw a picture
b. Watching a student make numbers with their hands
c. Watching a student throw a ball
d. Watching a student ride a bike

21. Which one of the following learning environments best allows for differentiated instruction?

a. Randomly placing the students with additional support needs throughout the classroom
b. Selectively placing the students with additional support needs throughout the classroom
c. Placing the students with additional support needs clustered together
d. Placing the students with additional support needs at the front of the class

22. Which of the following is the most appropriate use of technology to provide assistance with reading a story for a high school student who struggles with reading comprehension?

a. Allowing the student to use text-to-speech programs
b. Allowing the student to watch videos of the stories
c. Allowing the student to complete an online activity
d. Allowing the student to complete an electronic worksheet

23. Which of the following pieces of adaptive equipment could help ALL of the following students: one with hearing impairment, one with communication deficits, one with cognitive deficits, and one with fine-motor skills deficits?

a. A computer with a touch screen
b. A classroom amplification system
c. A large-print book/books on tape
d. A word processor with voice output

24. Which of the following classroom arrangements would be most appropriate for active teaching and learning?

a. Traditional rows and columns
b. Horseshoe shape
c. Clusters
d. Runway seating

25. When working with a group of eighth-grade students with writing deficiencies, which of the following intervention strategies would be most appropriate?

a. Providing a graphic organizer for the students to use
b. Modeling the writing for the students
c. Providing opportunities for the students to practice
d. Allowing students to collaborate with peers

26. A student was referred for a complete evaluation to determine eligibility for Special Education Services. Tests yield levels of cognitive and adaptive functioning. Which of the following is correct about how these results may be used?

a. They may be used in describing the student's Present Level of Functioning on the student's IEP.
b. They may be used as baselines to compare later scores in assessing program effectiveness.
c. They may be used to determine the student's levels for placement in Special Education services.
d. They may be used for any or all these purposes in making educational decisions for the student.

27. Which one of the following environmental factors is likely to have the greatest impact on students who receive special education services due to mental health concerns?

a. Sleep deprivation
b. Smoking
c. Exposure to toxins
d. Substance abuse

28. When teaching a small group of students with varying reading levels, what is the best strategy to ensure they are appropriately challenged?

a. Have the students read the same story, and give them comprehension questions at their ability levels.
b. Have the students read the same story, and have the more advanced students read aloud.
c. Have the students read different stories and work independently on their own questions.
d. Have the students read different stories, and have each student read their story aloud.

29. Clyde is 16 years old, has visual impairment, and reads on a first-grade level. What would be a good choice of materials for his teacher to provide him?

a. Large-print books on subjects relevant to teens
b. Children's books, which have large print and simple text
c. Regular library books with a magnifying glass
d. Large-print books with subjects geared to teens but with simplified text

30. Ms. Loomis is a teacher of LD (Learning Disabilities) students in Texas. This term she has had a new group of students referred to her for reading difficulties. She realizes that all of these students are English language learners (ELLs). Which statement about these referrals is most likely to be true?

a. These students will have reading problems regardless of which language they are reading.
b. The language acquisition process may well be the cause of these students' reading problems.
c. These students' reading problems are most likely the result of their learning disabilities.
d. These students' reading problems and their ESL status are most likely a coincidence.

31. Jared is a fifth-grade student with Down syndrome. Which of the following co-occurring conditions is Jared most likely to suffer from over the course of his life?

a. Heart diseases
b. Traumatic brain injuries
c. Diabetes
d. Depression

32. Marissa is an 11th-grade student who accesses special education services as a student with autism spectrum disorder. Which of the following lesson plan elements would likely be most beneficial in meeting her needs in her math class?

a. Providing a cross-curricular curriculum
b. Providing multiple tasks to complete
c. Providing multiple choices
d. Providing hands-on instruction

33. Sam is a third-grade student who struggles with writing. In diagnosing which part of the writing process he struggles most with, where would it be best to start?

a. Planning
b. Spelling
c. Mechanics
d. Semantics

34. When planning a lesson for a group of students with severe needs working on life skills, which of the following types of practice would be most likely used to ensure that they understand the material?

a. Guided practice
b. Collaborative practice
c. Independent practice
d. Student-led practice

35. Which of the following is true about stakeholder rights and an Independent Educational Evaluation (IEE)?

a. The testing is administered by someone who works outside of the school district.
b. The IEP team must accept the results of the IEE.
c. The parents must pay for the IEE to be conducted.
d. The parents must explain the reason for the IEE.

36. Which of the following is an example of how Maslow's hierarchy of needs can be applied to motivate students?

a. Using fear to allow students to find security
b. Establishing structure to allow students to find self-actualization
c. Setting goals to allow students to build self-esteem
d. Providing food as a reward to fulfill basic needs

37. Elise is a behavior specialist with a group of students who have various disabilities. One student has memory deficits. Another student has perceptual problems. A third student is diagnosed with difficulties in language processing. And a fourth student has IEP objectives to learn better problem-solving skills. In her research, which of the following would be a useful class of publications for Elise to read?

a. Journals of cognitive psychology
b. Journals of applied behavior analysis
c. Journals of the American Medical Association
d. Journals of neuroscience research

38. Which of these instructional strategies is mostly likely to enhance an LD student's social skills across different environmental contexts?

a. Assigning the student to be a peer tutor for another student
b. Assigning the student to be leader of a small group exercise
c. Letting the student practice by role-playing various situations
d. Cooperative designed practice with another teacher

39. When lesson planning for a life skills class for students with severe needs, which element is MOST important to include?

a. Objectives
b. Warmup
c. Direct instruction
d. Practical application

40. Tristan is a 10th-grade student with a specific learning disability in the area of reading comprehension. Which of the following examples would likely be the most beneficial in administering summative assessments to students like Tristan?

a. Administering alternate assessments
b. Administering assessments with modifications
c. Administering assessments with accommodations
d. Administering informal assessments

41. Mr. Hunt is a special education teacher with an elementary school class. He has one teacher's aide, one paraprofessional, and one parent volunteer, a mother, in his classroom. He uses peer tutoring methods as well. Three students, Marc, Fran, and Joe, have physical disabilities requiring assistance with snack time, bathroom breaks, and arts and crafts projects. One student, Clarence, likes to work alone on his math problems, but it is very important to him to have an adult check his work when he is done. Another student, Misty, is also very independent in her writing and art projects, but needs the emotional support of periodic encouragement on her progress and praise for her results when she is done. Daisy and Carmela are similar in age and educational level and are friends, but Daisy excels in math and is below grade level in reading, while Carmela reads above her grade level but is below grade level in math. Which scenario is an example of the best use of Mr. Hunt's human resources in his classroom?

a. The paraprofessional assists Marc, Fran, and Joe with snacks, bathroom breaks, and arts and crafts projects; the teacher's aide checks Clarence's work and reports to Mr. Hunt so Mr. Hunt can explain Clarence's errors to him and assign additional exercises; the parent volunteer encourages and praises Misty; Daisy and Carmela take turns helping each other in math and reading.
b. The paraprofessional checks Clarence's work, explains his errors, and assigns additional exercises; the parent volunteer takes Marc, Fran, and Joe to the bathroom; the teacher's aide helps with snacks; Daisy and Carmela take turns encouraging and praising Misty; Mr. Hunt helps Marc, Fran, and Joe with arts and crafts projects.
c. Mr. Hunt takes Marc, Fran, and Joe to the bathroom; the parent volunteer checks Clarence's work, explains his errors, and assigns additional exercises, and she helps with snacks; the paraprofessional helps Daisy with her reading and helps Marc, Fran, and Joe with arts and crafts; the teacher's aide helps Carmela with her math.
d. Mr. Hunt encourages and praises Misty; Mr. Hunt helps Marc, Fran, and Joe with arts and crafts and takes them to the bathroom; the teacher's aide helps Marc, Fran, and Joe with snacks; the paraprofessional helps Carmela with math and Daisy with reading; the parent volunteer checks Clarence's work, explains his errors, and assigns him additional exercises.

42. Which of the following is NOT a good example of adapting education to maximize the physical abilities of students with specialized needs?

a. Wyatt, who cannot write with a pen but can use his fists, answers test questions using a computer with a touch screen.
b. Fabian, who is blind and does not read Braille, listens to recorded test questions on a tape player with earphones, answering by pressing buttons on a counter.
c. Sue, who has impaired vision and impaired fine motor skills, takes a pen and paper test along with the rest of the students in her class.
d. Donnie, who is deaf, can participate in school fire drills because the school has both sound alarms and strobe lights.

43. Which of the following characteristics are most typical of a student diagnosed with autism?

a. Difficulty initiating and maintaining social interactions
b. Difficulty focusing and maintaining attention to tasks
c. Difficulty understanding abstract intellectual concepts
d. Difficulty sitting still and staying quiet for long periods

44. Jessica is a six-year-old kindergarten student. Which description may indicate typical language development?

a. She speaks in sentences of five to six words.
b. She has a vocabulary of 500 words.
c. She holds up her fingers to tell her age.
d. She uses phrases such as "me want"

45. After a parent requests a special education evaluation for his or her child, what would be the next step in the process?

a. Obtain consent and start the evaluation
b. Continue to provide responses to interventions (RTIs) until the team determines a need
c. Discuss some strategies the parent can use with his or her child at home instead
d. Ask the student's teachers whether or not they think an evaluation is warranted

46. Gerald is a fifth-grade student with a deficiency in reading fluency. How can the results of a diagnostic assessment in this area help to guide his instruction?

a. To figure out how much progress Gerald has made
b. To help decide which areas to focus on the most
c. To compare Gerald to his peers in the class
d. To understand which accommodations will work for Gerald

47. Intelligence quotients (IQ) tests can help determine whether or not students have learning issues connected with intellectual ability. What could be a disadvantage of this kind of test?

a. These tests cannot identify gifted students.
b. These tests cannot reveal student strengths.
c. These tests cannot measure certain skills.
d. These tests cannot identify future success.

48. Jerry is an eighth grader with multiple disabilities. Why would it be beneficial for a teacher to construct a new test to assess Jerry rather than using standardized testing data?

a. Students with multiple disabilities do not take standardized tests.
b. Standardized data likely do not assess what Jerry has learned.
c. Accommodations are not allowed on standardized tests.
d. Jerry will not need standardized testing data for college admittance.

49. Jacob is a third-grade student who scored one standard deviation below average in written expression on an academic achievement test. Which of the following best describes the likely next step for Jacob?

a. Jacob will be determined eligible for special education services.
b. Jacob will need additional tests specific to written expression.
c. Jacob will need to be administered an intelligence test.
d. Jacob will need to be evaluated for special education services.

50. Which one of the following strategies is likely to be the most beneficial for at-risk students with disabilities who struggle with mental illness?

a. Offering to seek help from the student's parents
b. Asking questions to seek more information
c. Allowing them to be alone with their feelings
d. Informing the school counselors of the concerns

51. When developing a lesson plan for a small group of students with specific learning disabilities in the area of writing, which one of the following is most important?

a. Ensuring that the students are accessing their accommodations
b. Ensuring that the students are working on their IEP goals
c. Ensuring that the students have access to the general education curriculum
d. Ensuring that the students have access to an alternate curriculum

52. George is a sixth-grade student with a specific learning disability in the area of written expression. Which of the following assistive technology devices would likely be least beneficial to George?

a. Graphic organizers
b. Proofreading programs
c. Frequency modulation (FM) listening systems
d. Word-prediction programs

53. The central problem in reading disability (RD) or dyslexia is thought to be:

a. With processing visual stimuli
b. With phonological processing
c. With aural and visual systems
d. With some unknown variable

54. African American students receive a higher percentage of special education services when compared to their peers of other racial or ethnic backgrounds. Which strategy can be MOST productive in applying this information?

a. Identifying African American students starting at an early age
b. Ignoring this information
c. Trying to maintain more of a balance in identification based on race
d. Being cautious about the evaluation process

55. What would be the best example of negative social influence?

a. Conformity
b. Independence
c. Compliance
d. Individualism

56. Bert and Nan are first graders receiving special education. They each have an IEP objective in reading/phonological awareness to produce rhyming words and distinguish rhyming from non-rhyming words. Bert is blind, and Nan has cerebral palsy with poor fine motor skills. Which of the following would be the best plan for both students to work on this objective?

a. Give both a worksheet with a list of word pairs and have each student circle the pairs that rhyme and cross through the pairs that do not rhyme.
b. Read a list of word pairs to both students and have each raise the left hand if the words do not rhyme and the right hand if they do rhyme.
c. Give Nan a worksheet with a list of word pairs, having her circle the rhyming pairs and cross out the non-rhyming pairs; read word pairs to Bert and have him raise his right or left hand to indicate if they rhyme or not.
d. Give Nan a list of word pairs, have her read them to Bert, and have him indicate by which hand he raises whether they rhyme or not.

57. What is true about materials to teach writing skills designed for students learning English as a second language (ESL) when applied with ESL students who also have LDs?

a. ESL textbooks do not afford enough practice of new material for ESL/LDs
b. The amount of material presented in an ESL lesson is appropriate for LDs
c. Graphics in ESL textbooks are just as visually appealing to LD students
d. The pace of instructional presentation with ESL-only is similar for ESL/LDs

58. Which of the following is not a way to teach children phonological awareness?

a. The jump-rope game "A my name is Alice and I live in Alabama and I sell Apples; B my name is Betty and I live in Boston and I sell Buttons...."
b. Playing the "I Spy" game while shopping, first looking for an "A" in the surroundings, then for a "B," etc., going through the alphabet
c. Singing "The Name Game" song "Shirley, Shirley, Bo birley, Banana fanna fo Firley, Fee fie mo Mirley, Shirley!" etc.
d. Reading Dr. Seuss books to and with children, e.g., Green Eggs and Ham, The Foot Book, Great Day for Up, and others

59. When working with a group of students with emotional disturbances, which of the following would be the best example of a measurable objective?

a. Measuring how much a student's behavior has improved
b. Measuring the number of outbursts that a student has
c. Measuring how well a student interacts with peers
d. Measuring how much work a student completes

60. Which of the following is the best example of maintaining a previously learned concept?

a. Giving students a daily quiz on vocabulary words
b. Giving students a study guide to practice vocabulary words
c. Giving students periodic questions on vocabulary words
d. Giving students a test at the end of the unit on vocabulary words

61. Eleni is a mainstreamed deaf student who uses American Sign Language (ASL). Which of the following actions is most appropriate to facilitate her communication with peers, faculty, and staff at school?

a. Teach Eleni speech reading so she can communicate with the hearing
b. Transfer Eleni to a school for the Deaf where everybody is using ASL
c. Teach Eleni's teacher, classmates and school staff some use of ASL
d. Teach Eleni Total Communication, which uses both ASL and speech

62. Which of the following is least accurate regarding reasons for educational inclusion of cognitively impaired students?

a. The majority of students are found to learn better in inclusive settings
b. Educational inclusion supports development of students' self-esteem
c. Inclusion teaches all students what equal rights and equal value mean
d. Federal law mandates that all students must have inclusive educations

63. Which classroom environment is most likely to support a student with ADHD?

a. Students with ADHD become bored easily so a classroom with distinct areas for a multitude of activities will stimulate her. When she loses interest in one area, she can move to the next and continue learning.
b. Students with ADHD are highly aggressive and easily fall into depression. The teacher needs to provide a learning environment in which sharp objects such as scissors, tacks or sharpened pencils are eliminated. This ensures greater safety for both student and teacher.
c. Students with ADHD are highly creative. A room with brightly colored mobiles, a multitude of visual and physical textures (such as striped rugs and fuzzy pillows) and plenty of art-based games will stimulate and encourage learning.
d. Students with ADHD are extremely sensitive to distractions. A learning environment in which visual and audio distractions have been eliminated is best. Low lighting, few posters and a clean whiteboard help the student focus.

64. An ORF is:

a. An Oral Reading Fluency assessment.
b. An Occasional Reading Function assessment.
c. An Oscar Reynolds Feinstein assessment.
d. An Overt Reading Failure assessment.

65. Susie has had severe school phobia for a long time, developing panic attacks when even approaching the vicinity of the school building or campus. She is starting therapy for this and is currently educated via homeschooling and tutoring. According to federal law, which is true about this situation?

a. Susie's current education violates the law by not being the least restrictive environment
b. Susie's current education conforms to legal definition of the least restrictive environment
c. Susie's problem does not qualify as an emotional disturbance under current federal laws
d. Susie's education should be in school because she qualifies for special education services

66. The ADA is:

a. The Americans with Disabilities Act
b. The Anti-Discrimination Act
c. The American Diabetes Association
d. The Alternatives to Discrimination Act

67. You have a population of multiply disabled students with profound intellectual disabilities. In IQ testing, the scores you will report are most likely to be ________________.

a. specific numbers below 55
b. below 20 but not specified
c. specific numbers below 40
d. below 30 but not specified

68. What legislation gives students and families increased protection in regard to the confidentiality of student records?

a. No Child Left Behind Act
b. Americans with Disabilities Act
c. Family Education Rights and Privacy Act
d. Human Equity Act

69. Phonemic drills are most appropriate for remediating which of the following?

a. Voice disorders
b. Fluency disorders
c. Language disorders
d. Articulation disorders

70. Among school-age children, reading disabilities are found in:

a. 10%
b. 20%
c. 30%
d. 40%

Refer to the following for question 71:

A teacher is concerned about three of her students. While they are enthusiastic about writing, they do not always recognize letters, confusing *b*, *d*, and *p*, or *e* and *o*. They do, however, know which sounds go with certain letters when they are orally drilled. When they write, they appear to be attempting letter–sound associations.

"Now I'm writing *M*," the teacher heard one boy say as he scripted a large *N* in the upper right corner of his paper. He studied it for a moment and added, "Nope, it needs another leg." The student then wrote an *I* beside the *N*. "There," he said. "Now you are an *M*. I can write the word *man* because now I have *M*." The child then moved to the lower left corner of the paper. "M-A-N," he said to himself, slowly pronouncing each sound. "I already have that *M*. Here is where the rest of the word goes." He turned the paper sideways and wrote *N*.

The second child sang to herself as she gripped the crayon and scribbled lines here and there on her paper. Some of the lines resembled letters, but few actually were. Others were scribbles. As she "wrote," she seemed to be making up a story and seemed to believe she was writing the story down.

The third child didn't vocalize at all while he worked. He gripped the paper and carefully wrote the same letter over and over and over. Sometimes the letter was large, sometimes tiny. He turned the paper in every direction so that sometimes the letter was sideways or upside down. Sometimes he flipped it backward. "What are you writing?" the teacher asked him. "My name," the child told her. The teacher then realized the letter was, indeed, the first letter of his name. She gently told him he had done a fine job of writing the first letter of his name. Did he want her to help him write the rest of it? "Nope," he cheerfully told her, "it's all here." He pointed at one of the letters and "read" his full name. He pointed at another letter and again seemed to believe it represented all the sounds of his name.

71. In the above example, the emergent writers are demonstrating their understanding that letters symbolize predictable sounds, that words begin with an initial sound/letter, and that by "writing," they are empowering themselves by offering a reader access to their thoughts and ideas. The next three stages the emergent writers will pass through in order will most likely be:

a. Scripting the end-sound to a word (KT=cat), leaving space between words, writing from the top left to the top right of the page and top to bottom
b. Scripting the end-sound to a word (KT=cat), writing from the top left to the top right of the page and from top to bottom, separating the words from one another with a space between
c. Leaving space between the initial letters that represent words, writing from the top left to the top right of the page and from top to bottom, scripting the final sound of each word as well as the initial sound (KT=cat)
d. Drawing a picture beside each of the initial sounds to represent the entire word, scripting the end-sound to a word (KT=cat), scripting the interior sounds that compose the entire word (KAT=cat)

72. Which of the following activities would be considered atypical cognitive development for a four-year-old?

a. Making up words and stories
b. Drawing pictures of objects
c. Pretending to read and write
d. Pointing to objects they want

73. Melissa is an eighth-grade student who receives services as a student with autism spectrum disorder. Which of the following co-occurring conditions is Melissa least likely to suffer from?

a. Anxiety
b. Epilepsy
c. Sleep conditions
d. Orthopedic impairments

74. Which of the following is most accurate regarding grouping strategies for teaching disabled and diverse students using multilevel instructional techniques?

a. These are best taught to the whole class
b. Small groups are the optimal arrangement
c. Multilevel instruction is best used in pairs
d. A range of grouping strategies can be used

75. Lead teaching, learning centers / learning stations, resource services, team teaching and consultation are all used in:

a. Innovative teaching
b. Strategic teaching
c. Collaborative teaching
d. Self-contained classrooms

76. Which of the following strategies would be the LEAST productive when working with a disabled student whom you suspect to be a victim of abuse?

a. Listening to the student and trusting what they say
b. Reporting the suspicion to child services
c. Continuing to teach in the same manner to maintain status quo
d. Asking the child for more details on the incident

77. Alex is a ninth-grade student who receives services as a student with a traumatic brain injury. In order to be eligible to receive services under this disability category, which of the following causes of the injury can be ruled out?

a. Birth trauma
b. Combat injuries
c. Violence
d. Sports-related injuries

78. Which of the following is the most correct statement about manipulatives for teaching math in grades K-12?

a. They are only efficacious when they are actual physical objects
b. They help make an abstract subject more concrete for learners
c. They are not yet available virtually on PC and so would not work
d. They actively engage student's less than traditional math classes

79. What is an example of a modification of the curriculum?

a. Access to textbooks with larger print
b. Access to a computer to type assignments
c. Access to manipulatives
d. Access to alternative books

80. The following teaching strategies all promote reading proficiency. Which one is more related to practice than to motivation?

a. Providing choices in the reading materials for students
b. Finding ways to make reading meaningful to students
c. Finding ways to make reading fun for students
d. Providing the students with many opportunities to read

81. Maria is a seventh-grade student with a specific learning disability in math and has failed three tests in a row in her general education math class. Which strategy would be least likely to help Maria improve her test scores in the future?

a. Asking her questions about the content
b. Discuss study habits she may have
c. Ask the counselors about changing classes
d. Updating the accommodations in her Individualized Education Program

82. At the beginning of each month, a student reads a page or two from a book he hasn't seen before. The resource teacher notes the total number of words in the section and the number of times the student leaves out or misreads a word. If the student reads with more than a 10% error rate, he is:

a. Reading with full comprehension.
b. Probably bored and his attention is wandering.
c. Reading at a frustration level.
d. Missing contextual clues.

83. When holding an Individualized Education Program (IEP) meeting with stakeholders, which method would be least effective in establishing rapport?

a. Facilitated meetings
b. Slide show meetings
c. Student-led meetings
d. Scripted meetings

84. Which of the following is an example of a preventive strategy for an at-risk student?

a. Short-term targeted intervention
b. School-wide behavioral supports
c. Intensive individualized intervention
d. Referral for Special Education evaluation

85. According to Bowen's Family Systems Theory, which is typical of the basic family relationship pattern when a child has a disability or impairment?

a. Excessive parental anxiety engenders a child with disabilities' corresponding excessive anxiety.
b. Parental focus on a child with disabilities increases the child's differentiation of self from family.
c. The child with the disability experiences less reaction than siblings to parental expectations.
d. Family tensions are less likely to be internalized or externalized by the child with a disability.

86. Jenny is a student teacher majoring in special education. She is working with a small group of students who are six years of age and have mild developmental delays. She wants to give them some Piagetian tasks to try. Which of these would be most appropriate?

a. Conservation of number tasks using rows of the same number of pennies, pebbles, or beads, arranged different distances apart
b. Class inclusion tasks using pictures and a 20-questions game to figure out which one the teacher is thinking of
c. Conservation of weight tasks using boxes filled with sand arranged differently, i.e., stacked or side by side
d. Conservation of volume tasks using liquid in differently shaped containers, i.e., a tall skinny container and a short wide container

87. Ross is a third-grade student who receives special education services as a student with an other health impairment due to ADHD. Which of the following strategies would likely be least effective for Ross?

a. Providing extra think time when asking a question
b. Providing one-on-one math instruction
c. Providing a setting with fewer distractions
d. Providing a model to demonstrate the task

88. Which of the following would determine a student to be ineligible for special education services as a student with a developmental delay?

a. A student with a delay in academic development
b. A student with a delay in social development
c. A student with a delay in adaptive development
d. A student with a delay in physical development

89. Which strategy would promote the safest learning environment in a sixth-grade science class with students with varying disabilities?

a. Displaying lab supplies at the front of the classroom
b. Displaying lab supplies at the back of the classroom
c. Locking lab supplies in a closet in the classroom
d. Locking lab supplies in a closet in a separate room

90. Which of the following is not true about students with visual perception LDs?

a. They have a higher rate of visual impairments than other students
b. They are likely to miss words, sentences, or paragraphs in reading
c. They can misinterpret facial expressions that transmit information
d. They can have trouble differentiating among visually similar letters

91. A second grader finds it impossible to remain in her seat. She wanders around the room, sprawls on the floor and rolls back and forth when asked to do math problems and jumps up and down when waiting in line. When the teacher tells her to sit down, she rolls her eyes in apparent disgust and looks to other students for support. When she finds a student looking back, she laughs and makes a face. The teacher has noticed when a reward is attached to good behavior; the girl is consistently able to control her actions for long periods of time. But when reprimanded without the promise of a reward, she becomes angry, tearful and pouts. This child is most likely manifesting:

a. Tourette's Syndrome
b. Attention Deficit Hyperactivity Disorder
c. Lack of sufficiently developed behavior and social skills
d. Psychosis

92. Which one of the following challenges is least likely to arise when collaborating with parents at IEP meetings?

a. Differences with regard to IEP goals
b. Differences with regard to accommodations
c. Differences with regard to attendance issues
d. Differences with regard to service delivery

93. Phillip is a third-grade student who has been struggling with reading fluency. The team has decided to evaluate Phillip for special education services and is considering the specific learning disability category. Which statement is true about this evaluation?

a. The team must have documentation of interventions that were implemented.
b. The team must administer an achievement test.
c. The team must administer an IQ test.
d. The team must consider state or local measures.

94. The current IDEA law defines a specific learning disability as a "disorder in one or more of the basic psychological processes involved in understanding or in using language, spoken or written, which disorder may manifest itself in an imperfect ability to listen, ____, speak, ____, write, ____, or to do mathematical calculations." Which of the following words does not fill in one of these blanks?

a. Think
b. Read
c. Spell
d. All do

95. Jason is a third-grade student with autism who excels academically but struggles with attention occasionally in the general education setting. Which of the following strategies will be most helpful in ensuring successful inclusion?

a. Placing Jason with the appropriate general education teacher
b. Pulling Jason from the room when he exhibits certain behaviors
c. Teaching Jason behavior strategies in special education
d. Placing a paraprofessional in Jason's class

96. Flash cards can be a useful math intervention for students who struggle with math fact calculations. When may the use of flash cards be inappropriate for students to practice?

a. When memorizing division facts
b. When students pass their math fact quizzes
c. When students are too young to read
d. When reviewing already known facts

97. Which of the following is least likely to explain the gender gap in identification of boys and girls for learning disabilities?

a. Boys are born with a higher tendency to develop a learning disability.
b. Boys are referred for evaluation more often due to a behavior bias.
c. Many tests are standardized for use with boys.
d. Expectations tend to be higher for girls.

98. What is NOT typically a responsibility of the special education teacher?

a. Managing paraprofessionals
b. Scheduling Individualized Education Program (IEP) meetings
c. Developing student class schedules
d. Supporting general education teachers

99. Which of the following characteristics of proficient readers *most* relies on metacognition?

a. Knowledge of correspondence between symbols and sounds
b. An understanding of the syntactic structures in reading matter
c. The ability to self-monitor to develop reading comprehension
d. Being knowledgeable about semantic associations in print text

100. Which of the following would be the responsibility of the school nurse with regard to students who receive special education services?

a. Serving as the case manager of the IEP
b. Ensuring that accommodations are put into place
c. Implementing mental health services
d. Providing health updates at eligibility meetings

101. Which of the following would be the best application of the cognitive learning theory in the classroom setting?

a. Repetitive practice
b. Research projects
c. Collaborative learning
d. Discussions

102. Freddy is a sixth-grade student who is struggling with his math class. Freddy's math teacher has provided some remediation to his work, but he is still struggling. What would be the MOST appropriate next step?

a. Evaluate Freddy for special education
b. Continue providing remediation
c. Attempt more intensive interventions
d. Remove the remediation and collect data

103. Which of the following would be the greatest disadvantage of co-teaching?

a. One teacher may teach more than the other.
b. The teachers may disagree on strategies.
c. The teachers may not be experts in certain subjects.
d. One of the teachers may not have much experience.

104. The left side of which lobe of the brain is most involved with mathematical calculations?

a. Parietal
b. Frontal
c. Occipital
d. Temporal

105. Which of the following best describes the most effective use of a developmental assessment?

a. As a norm-referenced scale
b. As a quick identifier
c. As a behavior rating scale
d. As an alternate assessment

106. Standardized tests can be a valuable assessment tool in evaluating students who receive special education services. When would standardized tests be inappropriate to use for data in measuring student growth or progress?

a. When evaluating students who take alternate assessments
b. When evaluating students new to the school
c. When evaluating students who have frequent absences
d. When evaluating students with accommodations

107. Brady is a second-grade student working on reading fluency. Which of the following would be the best example for a demonstration of learning at the end of the lesson?

a. Asking Brady to read a story and answer questions
b. Asking Brady to listen to a short reading passage
c. Asking Brady to read a timed short reading passage
d. Asking Brady to read a list of words with assistance

108. Which of these assistive technologies would be used by blind and visually impaired students?

a. Screen magnification
b. Text reader application
c. Screen reader software
d. All these would be used

109. Which of the following would least likely be one of the responsibilities of the school psychologist with regard to providing support for students with disabilities?

a. Providing mental health support
b. Administering IQ tests to students
c. Training staff on behavior plan implementation
d. Facilitating IEP meetings

110. Which would be the best use for the results of a student's curriculum-based assessment?

a. To determine which grade level a student performs at
b. To determine a student's percentage in a class
c. To incorporate into an Individualized Education Program (IEP) to show progress
d. To incorporate in a student's school file

111. What is a true finding about the qualities of students who read well?

a. They tend to focus on one central strategy for reading comprehension
b. Hypotheses, ideas synthesis, and conclusions are parts of their reading
c. Because they love to read, they do not need a reason for reading texts
d. They are not slowed down by having to reread previous sections of text

112. Jessica is a fourth-grade student with a specific learning disability in the area of reading comprehension. How might technology be incorporated into a reading lesson plan in order to meet her needs?

a. Allowing her to research a story on the computer
b. Allowing her to access to audiobooks
c. Allowing her to give a presentation instead of a reading
d. Allowing her to use her phone while she reads

113. Jasmine is a first-grade student with an emotional disturbance who is observed to assess her behavioral patterns. Which method of recording her behavior would likely be the MOST effective?

a. Discretely recording her behavior at random times in different classes
b. Recording her behavior at the same time and class each week
c. Asking Jasmine to help record her behavior
d. Having her teacher record each of her behaviors throughout the day

114. Researchers have found that to create a culturally responsive environment for enhancing reading comprehension, teachers should concentrate their endeavors on several elements, including teaching approaches and resource management. Which of the following is not another important element?

a. Positive classroom interactions
b. Curriculum and materials
c. Counseling and parent outreach
d. These are all needed elements

115. Which of the following best describes how technology can be included in a small group of students with disabilities working on reading comprehension?

a. Accessing audiobooks to listen to the story
b. Using computers to research the author of the story
c. Accessing speech-to-text software to answer questions
d. Using tablets to read a story and answer questions

116. Alison is a fourth-grade student with a speech-language impairment due to stuttering. Which of the following strategies would be least effective in providing a supportive classroom environment?

a. Having her skip presentations in which she has to speak
b. Having her collaborate with students that she is comfortable with
c. Having her pass when she is called upon in class
d. Having her sit near the teacher at the front of class

117. Which of the following is the best reason to implement cooperative learning into classrooms with students with disabilities?

a. Students are more likely to engage in this structure.
b. Students receive more support in these kinds of classrooms.
c. Students receive more instruction from teachers with this model.
d. Students are more likely to meet IEP goals in this environment.

118. Which of the following best explains why learning objectives should be time-bound?

a. Objectives should explain the progress toward achievement.
b. Objectives should require a reasonable amount of resources.
c. Objectives should lead to a desired goal.
d. Objectives should include a date in relation to the accomplishment.

119. According to research findings, which of these is not a recommendation for improving LD students' writing skills?

a. Teaching students to set specific, attainable goals for writing
b. Teaching students strategies for planning, editing, and revising
c. Teaching students to avoid using writing for content learning
d. Teaching students how to use PC word processing programs

120. Which of the following strategies would be most productive when differentiating the writing process for a student with a traumatic brain injury?

a. Allowing the student the use of a computer
b. Providing review sheets for exams
c. Reducing distractions on the student's desk
d. Slowing down the instructional pace

121. When interpreting the results of a norm-referenced test, how are the scores determined?

a. By comparing a student's score to a previous score
b. By comparing a student's score to other students that are the same age
c. By comparing a student's score to a standard deviation
d. By comparing a student's score to other students with disabilities

122. When teaching pull-out groups of elementary school students, which one of the following is a disadvantage to working with the students one on one rather than in small groups?

a. Students do not have access to their peers in one-on-one settings.
b. Students do not have access to the general education curriculum.
c. Students do not have access to their general education teachers.
d. Students do not have access to the special education curriculum.

123. Which of the following LDs is least likely to cause a student difficulty with math?

a. These all cause math difficulties
b. Language processing difficulties
c. Visual-spatial relation problems
d. Sequencing or memory deficits

124. What statement is accurate regarding research findings about methods for teaching reading fluency?

a. Assisted reading approaches have been found highly effective for fluency
b. Repeated reading and assisted reading approaches are mutually exclusive
c. Assisted reading methods work equally well one-on-one and in regular classrooms
d. Reading while listening is more efficient but unrelated to assisted reading

125. Sally is a preschool student who seems to be struggling in many areas. Which of the following can be beneficial in determining what kind of instruction would be most appropriate for her?

a. Intelligence quotient (IQ) assessments
b. Curriculum-based assessments
c. Alternate assessments
d. Developmental assessments

126. When writing learning objectives, the acronym "SMART" is often used. What do the letters in "SMART" stand for?

a. Systematic, measurable, attainable, reasonable, targeted
b. Specific, measurable, attainable, relevant, time-bound
c. Systematic, measurable, attainable, reasonable, tested
d. Specific, measurable, attainable, reasonable, time-bound

127. When does current federal legislation (IDEA 2004) require transition planning for students with disabilities to begin?

a. At age 18
b. At age 22
c. At age 14
d. At age 16

128. Emma is a nonverbal student who is assigned an oral presentation in her history class. Which of the following alternatives best allows her to access the curriculum?

a. Allowing Emma to present a slideshow instead
b. Allowing Emma to skip this assignment
c. Allowing Emma's aide to present the information
d. Allowing Emma to write a paper on a similar topic

129. Which technology application(s) can most help students learn math and science concepts?

a. Using software programs for modeling
b. CD-ROMs and Internet search engines
c. Email and word processing programs
d. Spreadsheet programs and databases

130. Which of the following is typically the most challenging in identifying a student who is an English learner for special education services?

a. The disability may or may not be related to language.
b. The Individualized Education Program (IEP) may not meet their needs.
c. Special education services may not be beneficial in English.
d. The student may already miss too much class.

Answer Key and Explanations for Test #1

1. D: Enthusiastically accepted. The adults discuss a background check and the possibility the teen might discover gardening is not for her and want to quit. However, this is most likely to occur early in her employment, giving the neighbor sufficient time to find another helper. The teacher is pleased because the girl will learn new skills through modeling and repetition. The mother is pleased because the experience will add to the girl's self-esteem as well as show her she is capable of learning. The elderly neighbor is pleased because she is both compassionate and truly needs help. The girl is delighted the neighbor recognizes her potential and sees her as valuable.

2. D: Although all of these choices could potentially be an issue for teachers who teach students with a wide range of needs, differentiating instruction is likely to be difficult. Differentiated instruction includes strategies to provide a curriculum that meets the needs of all of the students in the class. It can be difficult to differentiate or change the curriculum for so many students in one class in a way that meets their needs. Answer A is incorrect because IEP goals can be monitored at various times and not necessarily in one class period. Answer B is incorrect because the teacher will still need to provide the accommodations for each student. Answer C is incorrect because the teacher must still incorporate the assistive technology if a student needs it in class to access the curriculum.

3. B: Although all of these laws play a role in supporting students with disabilities, the Individuals with Disabilities Education Act (IDEA) governs special education services. IDEA is responsible for ensuring that students with disabilities are given their rights and supports that meet their needs. IDEA is instrumental and protecting not only students with disabilities but also teachers and other providers that work with students with disabilities. Answer A is incorrect because Section 504 is a civil rights act that protects everyone with disabilities, not just students. Answer C is incorrect because the Family and Educational Rights and Privacy Act protects students in the confidentiality in the protection of information related to that student. Answer D is incorrect because it is a civil rights act that gives the same rights to everyone regardless of disability.

4. B: Word prediction software (B) would be most indicated of the choices for a student having difficulty retrieving words stored in his/her memory. When the student struggles to recall a word, these programs can predict the next word to type based on spelling, syntax, and frequent or recent use. Voice recognition software (A) would be more appropriate for a student having difficulty with writing or typing, who can dictate spoken information that the software program then types. Speech output software (C) would be more helpful to students having difficulty reading text, by scanning it and reading it aloud with a synthesized voice, and those having difficulty with expressive language, who can type communications and have the voice synthesizer speak them. Spell checker software (D) helps students with sequencing disorders that affect spelling, visual perception disorders that can cause incorrect choices among similar-looking letters, and similar difficulties.

5. B: Although all of these choices can be helpful in ensuring that inclusion programs are successful, collaboration between teachers can best help students with disabilities access the general education curriculum. This collaboration can allow teachers to develop lesson plans and strategies to promote student growth. Without this collaboration, students with disabilities may not be as successful in their classes as they otherwise could have been. Answer a is incorrect because just meeting with the administrators may or may not change the inclusion programs at the school. Answer c is incorrect because although new assessments can help to measure growth, these may not always ensure successful inclusion. Answer d is incorrect because professional development in itself likely will not improve the inclusion model.

6. C: Assessing a young child for learning disabilities often leads to an incorrect conclusion because a student must be taught the subject before it is possible to assess her understanding of it. Intervention teaches the child specific skills to correct her misconceptions. If the intervention fails, assessment is the next step. Many experts recommend such assessment should not be undertaken until a child is at least six years of age.

7. A: Teachers will not always know a student's preferred communication mode. For example, deaf students often use sign language rather than speech. This is also true of learning modalities, such as blind students reading in Braille. Many teachers do not know either of these systems, but must be able to provide adaptations to meet these students' special needs. They can procure Braille texts without learning Braille, and they can obtain live, online, or video sign language interpreters without learning sign language. Teachers may also need to differentiate instruction based on gender because learning is not always the same for boys as it is for girls (B). Teachers are likely, especially with disability and diversity populations, to encounter age differences in one class (C). Learning English is not the sole responsibility of students (D) because many ESL/ELL programs and methods are available to teachers.

8. C: The WISC-IV (c) is not primarily* an assessment of adaptive skills. Rather, it is primarily an IQ test. The Wechsler Intelligence Scales for Children, Fourth Edition (WISC-IV) consists of a number of subscales testing different intellectual functions such as verbal comprehension, perceptual reasoning, working memory, and processing speed. These are all cognitive functions. *(Note: AAIDD's definition of intellectual disabilities, unlike IDEA's, includes receptive language, which incorporates verbal comprehension as a "conceptual" adaptive skill under its conceptual, social, and practical divisions of adaptive skills. However, the primary purpose of the Wechsler Scales is to test intellectual abilities.) The Walker-McConnell (a) Scales of Social Competence and School Adjustment are designed to assess adaptive functioning in the area of social skills. The Vineland (b) Adaptive Behavior Scales, as the full name suggests, are used to assess adaptive behaviors in people of all ages. Areas assessed include communication, daily living skills, socialization, motor skills, and an optional maladaptive behavior index. The SSRS (d) is the Social Skills Rating System. It gives measurements of positive social behaviors (including cooperation, empathy, assertion, self-control, and responsibility) and problem behaviors (including externalizing problems, internalizing problems, and hyperactivity). The SSRS also includes an academic competence scale, which is a brief measure of general cognitive functioning, performance in reading and math, and motivation and parental support. However, the primary purpose of the SSRS, as its name indicates, is to assess social skills, which are considered adaptive skills.

9. C: Schedule boards and communication boards allow people to communicate what their daily schedule is going to be and anything else they may need to communicate. Answer A is incorrect because audio players are for students who struggle with reading. Answer B is incorrect because listening systems are to help in reading a text. Answer D is incorrect because graphic organizers tend to be for those students who struggle with executive functioning.

10. B: Weak phonological skills (B) are characteristic of reading disorders. Phonological processing is necessary to being able to decode printed/written language (for hearing students) but is not classified as a sign of a writing disorder. Poor organizational skills (A) are common in writing disorders, making it hard for students to arrange their written thoughts in logical order. An inadequate vocabulary (C) is another characteristic of a writing disorder; students who know fewer words have fewer choices for composing written language to express their ideas or knowledge.

Weak planning abilities (D) are also identified in writing disorders. Like organization, planning is needed to execute written composition.

11. B: Curriculum-based measures are used in special education as quick, frequent assessments to determine whether or not students are making sufficient progress on their IEP goals. If a student with a specific learning disability falls behind on one of his or her IEP goals, the IEP team can review and implement measures to help the student before he or she falls too far behind. Choice A is incorrect because it refers to a type of norm-referenced test, where a student's scores are compared to similar students' scores. Choice C is incorrect because summative assessments at the end of a unit would typically be used to test mastery of curriculum. Curriculum-based assessments are formative assessments that only serve as progress trackers for class comprehension or IEP progress in the case of an individual. Choice D is incorrect because curriculum-based assessments do not always translate to official grades as they are simply a progress-marking tool.

12. C: It is important to move throughout the classroom periodically to ensure that students are on track academically and behaviorally while also keeping the teacher engaged. If the teacher stays in one spot during the entire class, students are more likely to act out or become a safety concern. Answer A is incorrect because just standing at the front of the class makes it difficult to monitor the progress of each student. Answer B is incorrect because walking around the classroom the entire time can potentially cause distractions to certain students. Answer D is incorrect because sitting with the students may be personable but could become an issue in accessing students who need support or may become safety concerns.

13. C: Approximately 2 to 3% of the population is classified as intellectually disabled and there are approximately 7 million intellectually disabled individuals in the United States.

14. C: It is very common for children with ADHD to also exhibit learning deficiencies in one or more areas. These students will often struggle to attend to their education, which causes them to fall behind and struggle with their learning. It is important to recognize and understand which disabilities a student may struggle with. Answer a is incorrect because learning disabilities are the most common co-occurring conditions with ADHD. Answer b is incorrect because speech problems tend to be more common in students with ADHD. Answer d is incorrect because fewer than half of students with ADHD also have conduct disorders.

15. B: A teacher's expectations are the desired result of his or her goals. On the other hand, goals are the means to obtaining the outcomes. For example, a goal may be to complete lesson one by the end of week one. This goal will determine the activities the teacher plans for that week. The teacher will also have the expectation that her student will complete and understand the lesson. Rules and procedures typically refer to acceptable behavior in the classroom. Effective classroom management will detail the rules of the classroom as well as the process to follow those rules. Taken together, well thought out goals, expectations, rules, and procedures will yield a well-run classroom.

16. B: Specific learning disability is a disorder that affects a person's ability to listen, think, speak, read, write, spell, or do math. Auditory processing disorder affects a person's ability to listen. Answer A is incorrect because speech or language impairment is its own category of disability. Answers C and D are incorrect because each of these falls under other disability categories and not specific learning disability.

17. A: Mr. John's lesson plan is based around a boys' basketball team. Ms. Deere objects to this because their class is coeducational, and girls are less likely to relate to scenarios about an all-boy team. Girls can also play basketball. The female students will probably feel left out when considering this scenario. Therefore option A is correct.

There is no reason students with hearing impairments could not play basketball with some accommodations, so they could relate to this scenario. Even if none of them has ever played basketball, they have probably all seen a basketball game by the time they are in high school (on TV if not live). Therefore option B is incorrect.

It is possible that Ms. Deere could resent Mr. John having written the lesson plan without her input. But this is not the most valid reason for her objection. If it were, the question would not state specifically that Ms. Deere feels the lesson is biased. Therefore option C is incorrect.

While the lesson plan does involve a physical education/sport activity, this does not mean that no academics are involved. The question states that the plan is for multimodal activities. The students will thus be doing a variety of activities using different media and modes of learning and expression. So academic exercises such as writing essays and taking quizzes or tests could easily be parts of the lesson plan. Therefore option D is incorrect.

18. A: Special education classrooms, once attended throughout the day by students with disabilities, are being used less frequently. Many students with disabilities are now in regular classrooms and may only spend a portion of their time in a special education classroom. This is also true for students with learning disabilities. Depending on the severity of the disability, a student may visit the special education room for a short period of time each day to receive additional support in his or her area of weakness. English and math are the most common subjects that students go to special education classrooms to receive instruction or help in.

19. C: Although all of these choices may be examples of some kind of formative assessment, observing her in class is most likely to provide the best data. Formative assessments are designed to assess what the student knows as the learning occurs. In order to monitor progress using formative assessments, it is important to take a look at the areas the student struggles in and if she is improving. Answer A is incorrect because interviewing a first grader like Andrea may not always provide the most accurate data. Answer B is incorrect because giving her academic probes most likely would not show whether or not she is developing on her social and behavioral skills. Answer D is incorrect because simply monitoring how she does on tests may not provide the whole picture in how she is developing overall.

20. A: When assessing a student for fine motor skills, it is important to take a look at activities such as drawing, writing, and using scissors. These kinds of skills are considered fine movements in that they are smaller movements that involve the hands, wrists, fingers, or toes. These kinds of assessments are important for determining whether or not a student needs additional support with a skill such as handwriting. Answer B is incorrect because watching a student making numbers with their hands is more of a tactile assessment. Answer C is incorrect because watching a student throw a ball would be looking at gross motor abilities. Answer D is incorrect because watching a student riding a bike would also be looking at his gross motor skills.

21. B: Although it may be easier in some aspects to have all of the students that need additional support together, this might create some issues. It is important to strategically place these students based on their needs and behavior. The teacher must be able to access these students in different ways that promote a safe and supportive classroom. Answer A is incorrect because randomly placing them could potentially create issues with their peers. Answer C is incorrect because if they are clustered together, they may feel singled out for being different from the other students. Answer D is incorrect because just putting them at the front could also isolate them.

22. A: Although all of these examples may help students who struggle with reading comprehension, text-to-speech programs are best in allowing the student to access the curriculum. Text-to-speech programs provide students with reading comprehension problems the opportunity to listen to the same story that the rest of the class is reading. It is important to provide students access to the general education curriculum whenever possible. Answer B is incorrect because watching videos of the story won't always give them all of the information that they need in the story. Answer C is incorrect because an online activity may leave out some of what the rest of the class is doing. Answer D is incorrect because electronic worksheets may be more beneficial after the story has been read.

23. D: A word processor with voice output can help the student whose hearing impairment makes speech more difficult and less clear; the student with other communication deficits impeding expressive language and/or speech; the student with cognitive deficits impeding speech-language development; and, especially with prediction as well as voice output, the student with fine-motor skills deficits impeding typing. The touch screen (A) would benefit students with fine-motor skills deficits and cognitive deficits more than the others. Classroom amplification (B) would help the hard of hearing student, but not others. Large print/books on tape (C) would benefit students with visual impairments and/or cognitive deficits more than the others.

24. C: Although all of these arrangements may have their benefits for certain students, clusters easily allow students and teachers to work together and move from group to group. Active teaching and learning is a beneficial strategy in that the students get to move around and work with different students. This cluster arrangement allows this movement for all students, including those with disabilities who may need to be accessed quickly and easily. Answer a is incorrect because traditional rows and columns tend to be more teacher-centered and do not allow for much movement throughout the room. Answer b is incorrect because although the horseshoe shape can provide space for the teacher to move, it doesn't provide as much freedom for the students. Answer d is incorrect because runway seating tends to be beneficial for teacher movement, but the students wouldn't be able to move as much.

25. A: Although all of these choices may be beneficial to certain students, providing a graphic organizer will likely produce the best long-term results. A graphic organizer can be beneficial for students who struggle with organizing their writing in that it gives them a framework for how to set it up. Many students struggle to organize their writing and stay on topic, and the graphic organizer is designed to help with this. Answer B is incorrect because simply modeling the writing likely is not enough support for many students. Answer C is incorrect because just providing opportunities to write without any feedback will not allow much improvement for the students. Answer D is incorrect because although collaboration can be helpful in certain circumstances, giving students the tools to complete work independently will help develop their writing skills.

26. D: These are all applications of evaluation results. All students determined eligible for Special Education services must have an IEP. In writing it, educators must include the student's Present Level of Functioning (A). To decide what the student needs to learn, by when, and how it will be measured, educators must establish baseline scores; retesting with the same instruments after a period of intervention and comparing scores will show if the intervention is effective (B) if scores improve. To make developmentally appropriate placement decisions, educators must know at what levels the student currently performs (C).

27. D: Substance abuse can be an extremely detrimental environment factor, especially for those with mental health concerns. Substance abuse can either lead to mental health concerns in family members, or it can be a cause of concern in the student. It is important to understand some of the causes of the concerns that students are reporting in order to intervene as early as possible. Answer A is incorrect because although sleep deprivation can impact students with mental health concerns, it likely does not have the same impact as substance abuse. Answer B is incorrect because smoking is likely to have more of an impact on a person's physical health. Answer C is incorrect because although exposure to toxins can be detrimental to a person's health, it likely has more of an impact on physical health.

28. C: When working with students with varying levels in the area of reading, it is important to challenge each student appropriately while also making good use of the time. Having the students work independently on their own stories and questions accomplishes both of these. Answer A is incorrect because some of the students may not be appropriately challenged if they all read the same story. Answer B is incorrect because the students who struggle more may not get enough practice. Answer D is incorrect because this may not be the most appropriate use of time.

29. D: Large-print books are a good idea for Clyde's visual impairment and subjects relevant to teens are appropriate for his age, but not for his first-grade reading level. Therefore option A is incorrect.

Children's books have the large print and simple subject matter Clyde needs but are not appropriate to his age. Therefore option B is incorrect.

With the availability of large-print textbooks, a magnifying glass is not the easiest way for Clyde to read. Having one would certainly expand the types of media he could see, and it would be beneficial for him to have it if he should want or need to see the small print in everyday media like newspapers and phone books. But for reading, it would not be as easy on his eyes as large print. Also, many books with regular size print will be beyond Clyde's first-grade level of reading comprehension. Therefore option C is incorrect.

Books in large print and on teen-related topics but with simplified text are the ideal combination for Clyde's visual impairment, age, and reading comprehension level. Therefore option D is correct.

30. B: The only way to identify a true learning disability with reading would be to test these students in reading both English and their native language. Without ruling out English as a second language being the source of their reading difficulties it is impossible to assume they all have learning disabilities regardless of language. Therefore option A is incorrect.

Because these students are all English language learners, it is more likely that this is the true source of their reading difficulties rather than learning disabilities. Therefore option B is correct.

Since English is a second language for these students, it cannot be assumed that the first or most likely cause of their reading difficulties is a learning disability. Therefore option C is incorrect.

It is so common for ELLs to perform less well in reading English than native English speakers that it is highly unlikely for reading problems and ESL status to be a complete coincidence with every student in the group. Therefore option D is incorrect.

31. A: More than half of individuals born with Down syndrome also suffer from heart conditions throughout their lifetime. Although many of these develop when they are born, heart conditions can arise at any time. This can lead to high blood pressure and an inability to get blood pumped to the heart. Answer b is incorrect because although traumatic brain injuries can happen in individuals with Down syndrome, they are most often caused by external factors and can happen to anyone. Answer c is incorrect because although diabetes is often diagnosed in those with Down syndrome, heart diseases are the most common. Answer d is incorrect because depression and mental health issues do not have quite the impact that heart conditions do.

32. D: Although all of these choices may be beneficial for students with autism, providing hands-on instruction would likely be the best option. It is important to provide different options for students to learn, especially those students who may struggle with the content. Giving students an opportunity to learn and demonstrate their knowledge using their hands can help them to retain the information. Answer A is incorrect because it may be overwhelming for some students to give them too much information at once. Answer B is incorrect because giving a student multiple tasks might be difficult if they are struggling with the first task. Answer C is incorrect because giving students choices is sometimes a good idea, but it might be a better idea to vary the teaching methods first to see how the student learns best.

33. A: In trying to discover where a student is struggling with writing, it is best to determine whether or not they are able to develop their own ideas. If students cannot come up with thoughts, they will be unable to write. Answer B is incorrect because spelling will be lacking if a student cannot come up with an idea. Answer C is incorrect because the mechanics will also struggle without being able to develop thoughts. Answer D is incorrect because semantics can also be affected by a lack of planning.

34. A: In order for students to learn from the lecture, it is important that they are able to practice it on their own. Students with significant needs may have a difficult time going straight from a lecture to independent practice, so guided practice is crucial. This gives them an opportunity to understand how to complete the practice. Answer b is incorrect because collaborative practice may not be as beneficial for students who need support from the teacher. Answer c is incorrect because independent practice for students with severe needs is a difficult task. Answer d is incorrect because student-led practice may not provide the results wanted without supervision from a teacher.

35. A: When parents request an IEE, the testing must be administered by someone that does not work for the same school district. Parents have the right to request an IEE when they do not agree with the results of a special education evaluation. The school must consider the results of this evaluation in order to ensure that it is providing FAPE. Answer b is incorrect because although the IEP team must consider the results of the evaluation, they do not have to accept them. Answer c is incorrect because the school district is required to pay for the IEE. Answer d is incorrect because an explanation is not required for the parents to request an IEE.

36. C: Setting goals for students in order to give them something to strive for and providing an opportunity for success can build self-esteem. Without this self-esteem, students will lack confidence and not be able to accomplish as much. According to Maslow's hierarchy of needs, human needs are arranged in a hierarchy and can provide value in seeking to motivate students. Answer a is incorrect because using fear is not a tactic that will allow students to find security. Answer b is incorrect because establishing structure, although it may be beneficial to some students, will likely not help those students find self-actualization unless creativity is allowed. Answer d is incorrect because providing food may not be the best long-term motivational strategy.

37. A: Journals of cognitive psychology are concerned with research in the study of memory, language processing, perception, problem-solving, and thinking. These are the exact areas in which Elise's students have educational needs. Therefore option A is correct.

Applied behavioral analysis means applying experimentally-derived principles of behavior with the goal of improving social behavior. Journals on this subject would not address the cognitive needs of Elise's students. Therefore option B is incorrect.

The Journal of the American Medical Association (JAMA) is a professional medical journal publishing peer-reviewed original medical research. It is a very popular journal among doctors. Its research articles would not typically address cognitive concerns like Elise's. Therefore option C is incorrect.

Journals of neuroscience research publish research results about the development, functions, and diseases of the nervous system, using molecular, cellular, and systems approaches. Diseases of the nervous system can affect cognitive processes. However, this research is not as directly related to studying the particular cognitive deficits of Elise's students as the journals of cognitive psychology are. Therefore option D is incorrect.

38. C: Letting the student practice by role-playing various situations (C) is most likely to enhance social skills across different environmental contexts, such as family, community, and business, instead of just school. Assigning the student to be a peer tutor for another student (A) is an excellent way to strengthen social skills and build self-confidence, but not necessarily across different settings. The student might get these benefits in the context of the specific academic subject or even of school, but not generalize them to other areas, particularly as LD students often have difficulty with generalization. Assigning the student to be leader of a small group activity (B) will also enhance social skills and self-esteem, but again, not necessarily across settings. Cooperative designed practice with another teacher (D) is an effective technique for improving social skills, but this option also does not afford as much generalization as role-playing different contexts.

39. D: For students who are learning about life skills, the practical application portion of the lesson is most important for them to practice their skills. Answer A is incorrect because although it is important for them to know the objective, the application tends to be more productive and memorable. Answer B is incorrect because a warm-up may not be practical for a group of severe needs students. Answer C is incorrect because life skills are often easier learned by doing rather than lectures.

40. C: In order to allow a student with a learning disability in reading comprehension to access summative assessments, it is best practice to provide accommodations. Summative assessments are designed to assess what a student has learned at the end of a unit of period of time, so it is important that they are properly assessed. Students with reading comprehension deficiencies, however, will need to access accommodations such as oral presentation of the text. Answer a is incorrect because alternate assessments are typically administered as standardized tests rather than summative assessments. Answer b is incorrect because students with learning disabilities typically do not access assessments with modifications. Answer d is incorrect because informal assessments are typically used for formative assessments.

41. A: The paraprofessional can assist with physical needs. The aide can check Clarence's work but should refer re-teaching and assignment of exercises to Mr. Hunt. The parent volunteer is a good choice to give Misty emotional support. Daisy and Carmela are the best choices for peer tutoring since they are very alike in age and grade level but are opposites when it comes to strengths and weaknesses in math and reading. Therefore option A is correct.

The paraprofessional can check Clarence's work but should not explain or assign exercises. The teacher should do these things. The parent volunteer may or may not be comfortable taking children other than her own to the bathroom. Misty may appreciate the peer approval implicit in receiving emotional support from Daisy and Carmela, but she may also prefer adult approval. Since Daisy and Carmela's strengths and weaknesses are so opposite and their other characteristics are so similar, their helping each other is a more directly beneficial use of peer tutoring. If both girls are busy supporting Misty they will have less time and attention to help each other and make their own progress. Although the teacher can give physical help with arts and crafts when he is the only adult in the class, since others are present who can help with this, he can do more teaching. Therefore option B is incorrect.

As the teacher, Mr. Hunt should not be taking students to the bathroom while the volunteer, the paraprofessional, and the aide do his teaching tasks. Therefore option C is incorrect.

In option D, Mr. Hunt is doing too many things considering how many helpers he has in his room. He is supporting Misty, helping the physically disabled students with arts and crafts, and also taking them to the bathroom. At the same time, the paraprofessional and the volunteer are doing his teaching tasks. Therefore option D is incorrect.

42. C: Wyatt cannot write but can use his fists, so a computer touch screen is a good way for him to record his test answers. This is a good example of adapting lessons. Therefore option A is incorrect.

Fabian cannot take a test visually, so his teacher has provided recorded questions and he presses buttons to record his answers. This is a good example of adapting lessons. Therefore option B is incorrect.

Sue cannot see as well as other students in her class and cannot use a pen as well as others. Yet she is taking a pen and paper test despite her visual and manual disabilities. This is not a good example of adapting lessons. Therefore option C is correct.

Donnie cannot hear the sound of a fire alarm, but the school has added strobe lights, which he can see, so he can participate in fire drills. This is a good example of adaptive education. Therefore option D is incorrect.

43. A: A prominent characteristic of autism is difficulty starting and continuing conversations, friendships, and other social interactions due to difficulty noticing and understanding others' emotional and social cues. Difficulty focusing and maintaining attention on nonsocial activities (B) and/or sitting still and staying quiet (D) are more characteristic of ADHD but are not generally problems for autistic students, who often focus exclusively on one solitary activity for long periods. Difficulty understanding abstract ideas (C) is more characteristic of intellectual disabilities. Autistic students without intellectual disabilities are more likely to have emotional/social impairments than intellectual ones.

44. A: By the age of six, typical language development will include speaking in sentences of about five or six words. By this age, children tend to have a vocabulary of 2,000 or more words, so answer choice B is incorrect. Children at age six are also expected to communicate their age orally rather than with their fingers, so answer choice C is incorrect. They also no longer say simple phrases such as "me want," which eliminates answer choice D.

45. A: According to the Individuals with Disabilities Education Act (IDEA), any time a parent formally requests a special education evaluation, the team must obtain consent and conduct the evaluation. Answer B is incorrect because an evaluation must be conducted whether the school believes it is needed or not. Answer C is incorrect because although it may be helpful to discuss strategies with the parent, this would need to be done in addition to the evaluation. Answer D is incorrect because the evaluation must be conducted even if the teachers do not think it is warranted.

46. B: Assessing a student using a diagnostic test in beneficial in providing a baseline score for what the student is able to do. Gerald's baseline score in reading fluency would give the teacher an idea of how fluently he reads and what areas still need to be improved upon. From there, the teacher can develop a lesson plan based on the results of this diagnostic assessment. Answer a is incorrect because it will not be until the instruction has occurred that progress can be measured. Answer c is incorrect because diagnostic assessments typically measure where the individual is rather than comparing them with peers. Answer d is incorrect because a diagnostic assessment likely would not provide information about which accommodations to use.

47. C: Although IQ tests can be beneficial for a number of reasons, they are limited in that they only measure certain subjects and skills. Because of this, they must be taken as part of a body of evidence that incorporates other tests and skills. Answer A is incorrect because IQ tests are one of the most popular ways to identify gifted students. Answer B is incorrect because these tests are designed to measure specific strengths and weaknesses. Answer D is incorrect because IQ tests often identify future student success in the areas tested.

48. B: Although standardized testing data can be valuable for certain students, many students with disabilities are learning an alternate curriculum. Alternative testing is available for some students, but teachers may find that constructing a new test is more beneficial in assessing what a student is capable of. This can be helpful in determining how much progress a student has made over the year or what the student still needs help with. Answer A is incorrect because students with multiple disabilities can still take the standardized tests with accommodations or alternative assessments. Answer C is incorrect because accommodations are typically allowed on standardized tests for students with disabilities. Answer D is incorrect because although Jerry may or may not attend college, standardized data can still be helpful.

49. A: Students that score at or below one standard deviation below the average level on an academic achievement test typically display a deficiency in that area. Because of this, a student like Jacob would likely be eligible for special education services as a student with a writing disability. Although the achievement test is just one piece of data that must be considered, a standard deviation below the average is considered a significant deficiency in that area. Answer B is incorrect because it is not likely that he will need additional testing based on these results. Answer C is incorrect because intelligence testing does not indicate whether or not a student has an academic skill deficiency. Answer D is incorrect because the academic achievement test is part of the special education evaluation.

50. D: Although each student may react differently to this support, it is important to seek help when it is warranted. Students that have or are suspected of having mental illnesses should be kept under a watchful eye, and help should be sought as soon as possible. For these students, it may be necessary to seek support from the school counselors even if the student is unaware. Answer A is incorrect because at-risk students may or may not want their parents to know about their concerns and this may trigger some strong emotions. Answer B is incorrect because asking too many questions might make these students feel uncomfortable. Answer C is incorrect because leaving them alone may not be productive if they are struggling and need some support.

51. B: When working with students in small-group pull-outs, it is important that the instruction is targeted to their IEP goals. Although each student may have a different goal, the teacher must plan the lesson in a way that fits in parts of each student's goal. Students may or may not have access to the special education teacher throughout the day, so it is vital to monitor and develop these goals when working with students in small groups. Answer A is incorrect because although it is important for students to access their accommodations, they would likely access these in the general education setting. Answer C is incorrect because students do not need to access the general education curriculum when working on IEP goals in the special education setting. Answer D is incorrect because students do not need to access an alternate curriculum to work on IEP goals.

52. C: Although these are examples of assistive technology devices, the FM listening system is typically used for students to listen to the speech of someone else. Students like George who struggle with writing will likely benefit more from devices that can help with the writing process. Assistive technology can be beneficial in helping students to access the general education curriculum despite their disability. Answer A is incorrect because graphic organizers can be helpful for students who struggle to start the writing process. Answer B is incorrect because proofreading programs can review what students have written. Answer D is incorrect because word-prediction programs can help predict what a student may want to write.

53. B: The central problem in reading disability (RD) or dyslexia is thought to be (B) with phonological processing. While reading printed or written language involves processing visual stimuli (A) as well, language is commonly learned through hearing (exclusive of deaf learners, whose lack of the usual auditory basis for language learning explains their reading challenges). Thus researchers believe phonological processing deficits to be more central to dyslexic difficulties than both aural and visual systems (C) for cognitive processing. Because this is the current thinking of neurobiological researchers, they do not primarily cite (D) some as yet unknown variable as being involved in dyslexia.

54. D: Overall, African American students have a higher likelihood of having a disability than others. It is important to not over or under-identify students simply because of their race, and we must be cautious of need rather than race. Answer A is incorrect because it is important to identify every student at an early age and not just a specific race. Answer B is incorrect because this can be important information to analyze. Answer C is incorrect because balancing out those who receive services based on race can lead to some students not receiving the services they need.

55. A: Social influences are everywhere around us, from the people we talk with, to social media, to entertainment. Conformity means changing one's behavior to be more like the norm. This can have negative effects. Changing to be like everyone else may mean that a person has changed a part of who he or she is just to fit in. Answers B, C, and D are incorrect because these all tend to be positive effects of social influence. Independence and individualism are the result of thinking for oneself. Compliance is the result of following the rules or guidelines.

56. B: Since he is blind, Bert could not read a printed or written worksheet or circle and cross out word pairs. Therefore option A is incorrect.

Both students could listen to word pairs read aloud. Even with poor fine motor skills, Nan has the gross motor skills to raise her hands. Therefore option B is correct.

As Nan has poor fine motor skills, she might have difficulty circling or crossing out words, especially since she is only in first grade. Therefore option C is incorrect.

Having Nan read a list of word pairs aloud to Bert would give Bert but not Nan the opportunity to show recognition of rhymes. Therefore option D is incorrect.

57. A: It is true that (A) ESL textbooks do not afford enough practice of new material for ESL/LD students. Students with LDs often need a great deal more practice than normally achieving students to learn new material, including learning a new language. It is not true that the amount of material presented in ESL lessons is appropriate for LD students (B). Typically, lessons for ESL students without LDs present too much material at once for students with LDs to handle. Textbooks for ESL-only students tend to use graphics that make them more visually interesting to engage students; however, these can be visually overwhelming and confusing to students with LDs, so it is not true that they are equally appealing to them (C). The instructional presentation for ESL students with LDs should not be similar to that for ESL-only students (D). Rather, it should be considerably slower for students with LDs to enable them to keep up with it. ESL-only lessons and texts tend to offer too much material, and too quickly, for ESL-and-LD students.

58. B: Playing "I Spy" looking for each letter in the alphabet (B) is not a way to teach phonological awareness, although it is a way to teach children alphabet knowledge. The jump-rope game "A my name is Alice" (A) is a way to teach phonological awareness by demonstrating similarities in initial word sounds within sentence patterns and using rhythm. Singing Shirley Ellis's song "The Name Game" (C) teaches phonological awareness by demonstrating similarities and differences in initial word sounds, discrimination among sounds, practicing rhymes, using repetition, and making it fun with the use of nonsense syllables and music. Reading Dr. Seuss books to and with children (D) teaches phonological awareness, as the author made extensive use of rhyming and repetition, reinforcing these with humor, imaginary creatures and names, and wonderful illustrations.

59. B: Although all of these objectives may be beneficial, they cannot necessarily be measured. The number of outbursts a student has over a given time period is something that can be calculated and measured. Measurable objectives should also be realistic for a student to achieve over a certain time period. Answer a is incorrect because it is impossible to measure how much a student's behavior improves without quantifiable data. Answer c is incorrect because it is difficult to measure social interactions. Answer d is incorrect because although it is possible to measure how much work a student completes, an objective must be more specific.

60. C: In order for students to maintain a skill, they will likely need to work on it periodically in order to remember it. Students likely do not need to work on it every day in order to maintain the skill — just once in a while. It is important for students to maintain their knowledge in order to continue building off it. Answer A is incorrect because a daily quiz is likely too much just to maintain the concept. Answer B is incorrect because just giving the students a study guide does not mean that they will practice the skill on their own. Answer D is incorrect because a test at the end of the unit does not allow them an opportunity to maintain the skill.

61. C: The most appropriate action would be to teach Eleni's teacher, classmates, and any able and willing school staff some use of ASL (c). While this might involve more effort, the other options may violate the IDEA law and/or her family's wishes. Teaching Eleni speechreading (a) could be objectionable to her parents if the whole family only uses sign language. Many people in the Deaf community reject speech as part of their Deaf identity and confine their communication exclusively to ASL. Transferring Eleni to a school for the Deaf where everybody signs (b) would make it much easier for her to communicate, but IDEA's Least Restrictive Environment (LRE) provision mandates students' placement in the environment with the fewest restrictions where they can still learn. If Eleni and/or her parents desired her to attend a school for the Deaf, then she would likely already be there. Teaching Eleni Total Communication (d), like teaching her speechreading, could be something that she and/or her parents do not want.

62. D: The least accurate statement is that federal law mandates that all students must have inclusive educations (d). Federal law does not mandate this, but what it does mandate is that all students must have the opportunity for the most inclusive education in the least restrictive environment (LRE) that still allows them to acquire a free and appropriate public education (FAPE). Some students may be unable to obtain such an education in an inclusive setting, which is why other educational options exist. Research has found that most students, however, do learn better in inclusive educational settings (a). Educators point out that inclusion is more supportive to cultivating students' self-esteem (b) than segregation, and that being singled out or deemed different has had negative impacts on many students' sense of self-worth. Special educators also note that all students can learn directly what equal rights and equal value mean (c) by being in inclusive settings: They can develop awareness, sensitivity, and tolerance for individual differences in such settings, learn that everybody has abilities and disabilities, and should work together.

63. D: Students with ADHD are generally extremely sensitive to distractions. A learning environment in which visual and audio distractions have been eliminated is best. Low lighting, few posters, and a clean whiteboard will help minimize distractions.

64. A: An ORF is an Oral Reading Fluency assessment. An ORF, also called Curriculum-Based Measurement (CBM) is a one-minute assessment in which the student reads a grade-level text aloud. The test supervisor notes errors the reader doesn't self-correct and the number of words read correctly.

65. B: It is true that (B) Susie's education fits the IDEA definition of the least restrictive environment (LRE). The LRE is the least restricted setting that still allows the student to receive a free appropriate public education (FAPE). Homeschooling or tutoring in this case is not more restrictive; the school setting is, because Susie's reaction to the public school setting completely interferes with her learning. The current arrangement does not violate the law by not being the LRE (A) because she would not receive a FAPE in public school with her current symptoms. It is not true that Susie's problem does not qualify as an emotional disturbance under federal laws (C): IDEA specifies not only that the student's educational performance is adversely affected, which it is, but also "a tendency to develop physical symptoms or fears associated with personal or school problems," and Susie has both. Another IDEA criterion for emotional disturbance is feelings or behaviors that are inappropriate under normal circumstances, which Susie's condition fits; and "an inability to learn that cannot be explained by intellectual, sensory, or health factors" additionally fits. "One or more" of these characteristics qualify as emotional disturbance under IDEA, and Susie has several. Although this qualifies Susie for special education services, this does not mean her education should be in school (D) if school is not currently the LRE.

66. A: The Americans with Disabilities Act. The ADA is a federal act prohibiting discrimination based on disability in the areas of employment, state and local government, public accommodations, commercial facilities, transportation and telecommunications.

67. B: Scores for this population are most likely (b) below 20 but not specified. This is because it is impossible with existing test instruments to specify exactly any scores lower than 20. This level signifies profound intellectual disabilities. Specific score numbers below 55 (a) would signify moderate intellectual disabilities, going down to 40. Specific numbers below 40 (c) signify severe intellectual disabilities, down to 25. Scores below 30 (d) are still in the range of severe intellectual disabilities.

68. C: The Family Education Rights and Privacy Act of 1974 protects student records. Under this legislation, only a student and his or her legal guardian may access the student's academic records. Third parties may be given permission to access all or part of these records; however, this permission must be in writing. Additionally, students have the opportunity to review their academic records and if necessary, make amendments in the instance of incorrect information. Information pertaining to the students' social security number, grades, GPA, and academic performance are protected by this legislation, as well as information about behavioral issues such as suspensions, academic dishonesty, and probation.

69. D: Articulation disorders involve distortion, omission, and/or substitution of speech sounds. Phonemic drills give students practice in producing sounds correctly. Voice disorders (A) are (outside of surgery) remediated by such therapeutic techniques as breathing support and audio feedback, among others, but not phonemic drills. Fluency disorders (B) such as stuttering are treated with a variety of techniques, including the Schwartz passive inhalation method, the Van Riper Program, Mark Power's method, Hollin's Precision Fluency Shaping, and many others, but phonemic drilling has no relation to fluency. Language disorders (C) involve difficulties with processing the language one hears, reads, speaks, and/or writes, and are remediated using many different strategies, although none of them include phonemic drilling.

70. B: Reading disabilities are identified in (b) 20% of school-age children. Ten percent (a) is only half the percentage of school-age children who are diagnosed with reading disabilities, while 30% (c) overstates this proportion by half, and 40% (d) is double the actual figure.

71. A: The next three stages are scripting the end-sound to a word (KT=cat), leaving space between words, and writing from the top left to the top right of the page and from top to bottom. Each of these steps is progressively more abstract. Scripting the end-sound to a word helps a young writer recognize that words have beginnings and endings. This naturally leads to the willingness to separate words with white space so that they stand as individual entities. Once this step is reached, the child realizes that in English, writing progresses from left to right and from the top of the page to the bottom.

72. D: Children at the age of four will no longer just point to the objects that they want in most cases. These children are able to communicate verbally and ask for what they want with words. If a child is still pointing to objects that they want at the age of four, this may indicate some kind of developmental delay. Answer A is incorrect because making up words and stories is considered typical development. Answer B is incorrect because drawing pictures of objects that they see is common with four-year-olds. Answer C is incorrect because pretending is also an activity that comes with the development of a child who is four years old.

73. D: Although students with autism spectrum disorder may suffer from orthopedic impairments at a higher rate than their peers, this is not typically one of the co-occurring conditions. Students with autism tend to suffer from many mental and physical conditions. According to Autism Speaks, the largest autism advocacy organization in the United States, many of these conditions co-occur with students diagnosed with autism. Answer A is incorrect because anxiety is common with students with autism. Answer B is incorrect because epilepsy is also a commonly co-occurring condition with autistic students. Answer C is incorrect because sleep conditions are also very common.

74. D: Multilevel instructional practices can be used in various grouping arrangements, including whole class (A), small group (B), and paired (C) contexts; no one of these is better than the others. When arrangements other than whole class instruction are used, the smaller groups of students are typically still mixed in character rather than being homogeneous. Multilevel instruction is based on the principle that all students have a chance to access suitable instruction and to get support from their teachers and classmates.

75. C: Collaborative teaching. Classrooms with a lead teacher often include a specialized teacher to listen to the lesson then work with special needs children. Other methods are: learning centers or stations in which collaborating teachers are responsible for different areas, assigning special needs students into a resource room, team teaching and/or consultation by the special education teacher to the classroom teacher.

76. D: When working with a student that is suspected to be a victim of abuse, it is not always beneficial to dig deep into what has occurred. Although some students may be open to sharing what has happened to them, others may not, and they might feel pressured. Many students with disabilities are victims of neglect and abuse and they have a higher likelihood than their peers of being victims. Additionally, the role of a teacher or other staff member is usually to be a reporter of suspected abuse and neglect, but not an investigator. Teachers and staff should remain anonymous if possible when reporting suspicion to maintain trust and a safe position. Answer A is incorrect because listening to the student to hear what they have to say may help calm them and help discover information. It is not advisable for teachers to look for more information when suspecting abuse or neglect, but any information that the student readily gives can be included in a report of suspicion to help with any subsequent investigations. Answer B is incorrect because reporting the incident to child services is mandatory. Answer C is incorrect because continuing to teach them as usual will provide normalcy for the students and will help the student feel safe rather than in the spotlight. Victims of abuse often struggle with shame and guilt, so it is important for teachers to not draw unwanted attention to the student in normal environments like the classroom.

77. A: According to IDEA, birth trauma would not be considered one of the causes of traumatic brain injury. Students with birth trauma would likely be considered under a different eligibility category. Students who receive services under the traumatic brain injury category will typically have a medical diagnosis of a traumatic brain injury. Answer b is incorrect because combat injuries can be one of the causes of traumatic brain injuries, even at a young age. Answer c is incorrect because violence is often associated with students who are impacted by traumatic brain injuries. Answer d is incorrect because sports-related injuries can also cause damage to the brain and cause traumatic brain injuries.

78. B: Manipulatives make the abstract concepts of mathematics more concrete for students, making them good choices for students whose levels of cognitive development allow more concrete than abstract thought. Historically they have been physical objects, but, this is no longer necessary with computer technology (A). Virtual manipulatives are available and are also found effective (C). For example, the University of Utah has developed (and continues to develop) the National Library of Virtual Manipulatives through a grant from the National Science Foundation. While they cannot handle virtual manipulatives like physical ones, students can still see and manipulate objects onscreen to see concept relationships and applications more concretely. These virtual programs are interactive and promote students' active engagement more than traditional math lessons typically do (D).

79. D: Modifications of the curriculum alter the curriculum that is being taught, and these students are expected to complete assessments different than that of their peers. Access to alternative books changes what the student is learning and therefore would change the expectations for the assignment. Answers A, B, and C are all accommodations that allow students to access the same curriculum as their peers with alterations to how the material is presented. Textbooks with large print, computers for typing, and manipulatives are all accommodations to allow students to access the curriculum.

80. D: Providing students with many opportunities to read encourages reading proficiency by allowing them more reading practice. Providing the students with choices of reading materials (A) has also been shown to enhance their motivation to read because they have more control and choice than they do when reading only teacher-chosen materials, and because they can choose to read something that is personally appealing to them. When teachers can show students what is meaningful in what they read, students are more interested in reading (B). Teachers can also enhance students' motivation to read by making the activity fun (C).

81. A: Reviewing the content with her if she is already struggling with the material may prove to be ineffective to a student with a learning disability. There is likely a reason she is struggling with these tests. Answer B is incorrect because it is possible that Maria does not know how to study for a math test. Answer C is incorrect because changing classes would likely improve her grade if she were to move to a lower class. Answer D is incorrect because she may need to access accommodations that weren't previously in her Individualized Education Program.

82. C: Reading at a Frustration reading level. At a Frustration reading level, a student is unable to unlock meaning from a text regardless of teacher support or strategies. The reader is at this level when he has less than 90% accuracy in word recognition and less than 50% in comprehension, retelling a story is illogical or incomplete and the student cannot accurately answer questions about the text.

83. D: If the IEP meeting is already scripted, it does not provide each of the stakeholders with an opportunity to provide input and share their side of the story. Answer A is incorrect because facilitated meetings are a great way to make everyone feel included and have a say. Answer B is incorrect because a slide show presentation can be more entertaining than simply reading from the IEP. Answer C is incorrect because a student-led meeting heavily includes the student and allows him or her to truly be the center of the meeting.

84. B: Many instructional models use a progressively tiered system. The first tier typically consists of general education classroom core instruction and school-wide (or school system/district-wide) behavioral supports, which all students receive as a way to prevent school problems before they start. Students not succeeding receive second-tier, short-term targeted interventions (A). Those whom this does not help then receive third-tier, more intensive, more individualized interventions (C). Only if the student continues to fail with these do educators refer them for Special Education evaluation (D).

85. A: The more the parents focus their anxiety and worry on a child with an impairment, the more the child in turn focuses anxiety and worry on the parents. The parents' greater focus of anxiety on one child decreases that child's differentiation of self from the family rather than increasing it (B). The child with the disability becomes more reactive than his/her siblings to parental expectations, needs, and attitudes, not less (C). The child with a disability is more likely to internalize or externalize family tensions, not less (D).

86. A: According to Piaget, elementary-school-age children are in the stage of concrete operations. They can understand mental operations and their reversibility for the first time. Piaget said that children develop certain conservation skills earlier and others later. Conservation of number develops earliest, usually around ages five to seven years. The children in this question have mild developmental delays. So it can be expected that some of them may have developed this understanding and some have not. This would be a good task to offer them at their age. Therefore option A is correct.

Class inclusion is typically acquired around the age of seven or eight years. These children are only six and also have mild developmental delays, so they may be a year or two behind other children in cognitive development. In tests with the 20-questions game, children six to eight with normal cognitive development would simply guess (e.g., "Is it a banana?"), whereas children aged nine to eleven would think in terms of categories (e.g., "Is it something you eat?"), showing the ability of classification. A class inclusion task for six-year-olds with mild developmental delays would be too advanced and they would probably all fail at it. Therefore option B is incorrect.

Conservation of weight usually develops around the ages of nine to ten years. This would be beyond the development of cognitively average six-year-olds, let alone those with mild developmental delays. Therefore option C is incorrect.

Conservation of volume is typically attained around the ages of twelve to fourteen according to Piaget. It would be far beyond the cognitive abilities of six-year-olds. Therefore option D is incorrect.

87. B: Although individualized instruction is helpful for many students, including students with a disability such as ADHD, it is the least effective for targeting the specific educational needs of students with ADHD. Many students with ADHD will simply need support in the classroom or in a separate setting that reduces opportunities for distraction. It is worth noting that strategies such as small-group instruction or separation from the rest of the class can be considered a restriction that violates the right to the least restrictive environment. Instead, a teacher should seek to provide support within the student's primary class if possible. Answer a is incorrect because extra think time can allow students to collect their thoughts before they speak. Answer c is incorrect because settings with fewer distractions allow these students to concentrate. Answer d is incorrect providing a model to demonstrate can allow the student to see how something is done before doing it.

88. A: A student with an academic delay would not be eligible for the "developmental delay" category, according to IDEA. The category includes many areas, but it does not specify academics as one of them. Instead, the criteria include cognitive development but do not use the term "academic development." Answer B is incorrect because a student with a social development delay would be eligible according to IDEA criteria. Answer C is incorrect because adaptive delays are also listed under the IDEA definition. Answer D is incorrect because a delay in physical development would also determine a child to be eligible as a student with a developmental delay.

89. C: To organize the classroom in the safest way possible, it is best to keep items like lab supplies hidden from the students. This way, students are not tempted to play with the lab supplies when they are not allowed to. Answers A and B are incorrect because having the supplies displayed can be dangerous for impulsive students or those with behavior problems. Answer D is incorrect because, although it is a good idea to have the supplies locked away, it is best practice to have them in a more accessible location.

90. A: It is not true that students with visual perception LDs (A) have a higher rate of visual impairments than other students. Difficulties with visual perception occur in the brain areas that interpret visual signals, not with the sensory ability of eyesight. Students with visual perception problems can have perfect vision. This LD makes students likely to miss words, sentences, or entire paragraphs when they are reading (B). Students with this type of LD can also misunderstand others' facial expressions that communicate such things (C) as disbelief, approval, boredom, or indicating that a conversation is over. Another common effect of a visual perception LD is having difficulty telling apart similar-looking letters (D), numbers, characters, or symbols. Perceiving letters backwards or distorted also frequently occurs with this type of LD.

91. C: The child may or may not be hyperactive, but the fact that she can control her behavior for extended periods if a reward is involved suggests the child is overly indulged outside of class. In addition, she appears to act out in an effort to seek peer admiration; this excludes the possibility of Tourette syndrome and Attention Deficit Hyperactivity Disorder. In the first case, she would be unlikely to seek approval. In the second, she would be unlikely to be able to control herself under certain circumstances. There is nothing in her behavior to suggest psychosis.

92. C: Although parents may discuss some of the issues they have with their child's attendance at the IEP meeting, this is not typically discussed at the meeting. Differences that arise from the IEP meeting will be typically stem from the IEP itself. Because there is no section in the IEP that specifically discusses attendance issues, this is the least likely issue to arise. Answer A is incorrect because it is common for the parents and teacher to have differences with regard to the student's IEP goals. Answer B is incorrect because parents may disagree about some of the accommodations that their child has access to. Answer D is incorrect because some parents may also have differences of opinion regarding the service delivery section of the IEP.

93. A: To consider a student eligible for special education services as a student with a specific learning disability, there must be documentation of interventions that have been attempted to show the student is not achieving growth. Answer B is incorrect because although an achievement test might be helpful, it is not mandatory. Answer C is incorrect because IQ tests do not typically show academic performance. Answer D is incorrect because these data aren't necessary in the process but can be useful.

94. D: All do (D). IDEA's definition of specific learning disability is a "disorder in one or more of the basic psychological processes involved in understanding or in using language, spoken or written, which disorder may manifest itself in an imperfect ability to listen, think (A), speak, read (B), write, spell (C), or to do mathematical calculations." Therefore there is not one of these words that does not fill in the blanks correctly.

95. D: For students who struggle with behavior, it is often helpful to have someone in the classroom to help support the general education teacher. In order to ensure inclusion for students, it is important that they have access to the general education curriculum as often as possible. Having a paraprofessional in the class to support the student allows them to access the curriculum and have support when they need it. Answer A is incorrect because although placing a student with a specific teacher can be helpful, support should still be in place no matter who the teacher may be. Answer B is incorrect because if a student is constantly pulled from the classroom, they will miss the instruction. Answer C is incorrect because although teaching him strategies can help, it may be more beneficial for him to be in the class learning with his peers.

96. D: If students have already memorized the facts on flash cards, it may be considered a waste of time to continue to review them over and over again. Answer A is incorrect because flash cards can be great to help memorize division facts. Answer B is incorrect because flash cards can still be used with problems students struggled with even if they passed a test. Answer C is incorrect because even if students are too young to read, they can still practice math facts.

97. D: Boys are identified with learning disabilities at a higher rate than girls but not likely because expectations are higher for girls. Although some teachers may have biases and expectations for girls and boys, there is no evidence to suggest that this had led to underidentifying girls. It is, however, important to identify students for special education evaluations for the right reasons. Answer A is incorrect because studies have shown that boys are born with a higher likelihood of developing a disability. Answer B is incorrect because boys tend to exhibit more negative behaviors in the classroom, and these can lead to special education referrals. Answer C is incorrect because studies have shown that some of the tests are standardized for boys and do not always take girls into consideration.

98. C: Typically, the special education teacher will collaborate with school counselors and administrators about what the best placement for students may be, but they aren't solely responsible for coming up with the class schedule. Answer A is incorrect because managing paraprofessionals is an important task for the special education teacher. Answer B is incorrect because scheduling IEP meetings with the parent is also an important task. Answer D is incorrect because it is important for the special education teacher to help support the general education teacher about ways to help students with IEPs.

99. C: Metacognition is the knowledge and regulation of one's own cognitive processes, and is often described as "thinking about thinking." Proficient readers most rely on metacognition to engage in self-monitoring while they read, thus promoting comprehension. Knowing how spelling and speech sounds correspond with one another (A), understanding word order and sentence structure in reading material (B), and recognizing the meanings in what they read (D) are all specific aspects of processing print structures used by proficient readers.

100. D: The school nurse may have many roles and responsibilities, but one of them is to provide a health update for each eligibility meeting. It is important that the student's health concerns are updated to determine what impact they might have on a student's access to education. The school nurse may have more involvement for certain students on IEPs than others but is typically involved with each one at some point. Answer A is incorrect because the special education teacher typically serves as the case manager. Answer B is incorrect because the special education teacher also ensures that accommodations are put into place. Answer C is incorrect because the school counselor or social worker will likely implement mental health services.

101. D: The cognitive learning theory states that learning occurs through a process in which people internalize their thoughts in order to provide information. Discussions are an example of how the internalization of information can be shared with others. Understanding the cognitive learning theory can help one understand how learning occurs. Answer a is incorrect because repetitive practice is an example of an application of the behaviorist learning theory. Answer b is incorrect because research projects are an example of the application of the constructivist learning theory. Answer c is incorrect because collaborative learning is also an example of the constructivist learning theory in which knowledge is constructed based on individual experiences.

102. C: Before being referred for special education services, the team must provide intensive interventions to see how Freddy responds to those. Answer A is incorrect because the team must provide more support before evaluating for special education. Answer B is incorrect because continuing to provide the remediation likely will not work as there have been no improvements.

Answer D is incorrect because removing the remediation would likely cause Freddy to struggle more.

103. B: Although all of these choices could be potential conflicts in the co-teaching model, disagreeing on strategies is likely the greatest disadvantage. When teachers collaborate to teach a class, the general education teacher and special education teacher may have different approaches to certain topics and tasks. This may lead to some conflicts about the instructional strategies or how some of the students learn best. Answer A is incorrect because typically co-teaching will involve one teacher teaching more than the other. Answer C is incorrect because it is best to collaborate in subjects that teachers are familiar with in order to provide students with the best possible instruction. Answer D is incorrect because even if one teacher does not have as much experience, it is still possible to collaborate and learn from one another.

104. A: Neuroimaging studies find that the left side of the (A) parietal lobe, located behind the frontal lobe at the back of the top of the brain, is most involved with mathematical calculations. The frontal (B) lobe is involved with speech, emotions, and executive functions such as solving problems, making decisions, and planning. The occipital (C) lobe is at the back of the brain and is responsible for the processing of information received through the sense of vision. The temporal (D) lobe is below the frontal and parietal lobes and is involved with aspects of speech, memory, perceiving and identifying auditory stimuli (sounds), and other functions. Damage in the parietal-temporal area can cause deficits in digit span and verbal memory.

105. A: Developmental assessments are designed to find strengths and weaknesses in young students who may be exhibiting some delays. In order to do this, students are compared with what the average student is capable of doing in many developmental categories. These assessments can be effective in intervening in students early who may be struggling. Answer B is incorrect because a quick identifying assessment that would be used is typically referred to as a screener. Answer C is incorrect because a behavior rating scale typically identifies just the behavior of students of all ages. Answer D is incorrect because an alternative assessment is typically used for students with disabilities who cannot access standardized tests.

106. A: Students who are eligible to take alternate assessment due to the impact of their disability will likely not take the same standardized tests as their peers. These students will likely struggle with the standardized test, and the alternate assessment will provide more valuable information. Answer B is incorrect because students new to the school can still take standardized tests as they are the same for every grade level. Answer C is incorrect because although students with absences may struggle more with the test, it is still valuable in determining what they know. Answer D is incorrect because students with accommodations can access those for standardized tests.

107. C: The demonstration of learning should show whether or not a student met the daily objective. For students working on reading fluency, reading a short passage that is timed will show if they met the daily reading fluency objective. This is designed to be a quick assessment without any assistance from the teacher. Answer A is incorrect because reading a short story and answering questions may not be the best way to assess reading fluency. Answer B is incorrect because listening to a passage does not allow Brady to demonstrate his reading fluency ability. Answer D is incorrect because the demonstration of learning is designed to be an individual activity without assistance.

108. C: Screen reader software can read aloud information from a computer screen, not only in documents, but also desktop icons, menu options, error messages, dialog boxes, and on websites and pages, to assist students with vision problems. Screen magnification software (A) can be used by visually impaired students but not by blind students. Text reader software applications (B) are not primarily intended for or used by blind or visually impaired students. They read text aloud as it is being typed on the keyboard, and read aloud electronic text as in emails and word processing documents; they are used more by ESL students, students with learning disabilities, and students with other reading difficulties than by people with visual impairments. Therefore students with visual impairments would not use all of these (D).

109. D: Although school psychologists may facilitate IEP meetings in certain cases, the special education teacher typically runs these meetings. The school psychologist may be involved in many phases of the meeting including assessing students and consulting with general and special education teachers. The special education teacher serves as the case manager in most instances, however, and is responsible for scheduling and running the IEP meetings. Answer A is incorrect because school psychologists will often provide mental health support to students. Answer B is incorrect because school psychologists are also often responsible for administering different kinds of tests including IQ assessments. Answer C is incorrect because school psychologists can also assist special education teachers in training staff on implementing behavior support.

110. C: Curriculum-based assessments can be valuable tools in monitoring a student's progress compared with what his or her IEP goals are. These are typically quick assessments that give the teacher data right away. Answer A is incorrect because curriculum-based assessments typically compare students to their own growth rather than determine grade level. Answer B is incorrect because curriculum-based assessments are separate from classroom grades. Answer D is incorrect because it would likely not end up in a student's school file.

111. B: Proficient readers formulate hypotheses, incorporate ideas into larger constructs, and generate conclusions as they read. They also employ a variety of strategies to achieve comprehension of what they read rather than just one strategy (A). While proficient readers may love to read, one of their various strategies is also to understand the reason for reading a particular text, which is needed (C) to provide them with a focus when reading it. Another strategy used by students who read well is to reread or skim passages they have already read to increase their comprehension of them; they do not avoid this to prevent slowing their reading progress (D).

112. B: Audiobooks can be beneficial to students who struggle with reading comprehension. This is a good opportunity for someone like Jessica to take in the content without having to struggle with the reading. Using this technology can be beneficial to students who are still learning to read. Answer A is incorrect because simply researching her topic may not help her with reading. Answer C is incorrect because although giving a presentation may be beneficial, it is still important for her to read the content. Answer D is incorrect because allowing her to use her phone may be too distracting.

113. A: To assess Jasmine's behavioral patterns, it is best to record her behavior during random times when she may or may not know she is being observed. This will provide a true indication of her behavior and give results from different parts of her day and in different classes. Answer B is incorrect because if her behavior is recorded at the same time, she will catch on and change her behavior. Answer C is incorrect because although having her help may be beneficial, it may not always provide the most reliable results. Answer D is incorrect because it would be a difficult task for her teacher to record everything and some behavior might be missed.

114. D: These are all needed elements (d). By promoting positive classroom interactions (a), teachers can improve students' confidence, willingness to participate, and engagement in instruction. By paying attention to the curriculum and materials they use (b), teachers can facilitate learning by making it more meaningful to students. For example, they can provide reading material with which students can identify personally through themes they recognize, validating their cultural identity. Counseling (c) provides students with the opportunity to express wants, needs, and feelings, even as it allows teachers to help students cope with these, gain insights, and adjust to environmental differences. Parent outreach (also c) gets families involved in students' education and provides teachers with valuable information about students' learning problems, learning styles, strengths, interests, and strategies that have and have not worked at home and/or in previous schools.

115. D: Although all of these choices may be beneficial for students who struggle with reading comprehension, using a tablet allows the student to practice reading and answering questions. It is important for students to practice these skills as much as possible in order to improve them. For many students, using a tablet to read a story may yield better results than simply reading the story and taking a quiz or test. Answer a is incorrect because although audiobooks can be a useful accommodation, it would likely be more productive to have students practice the skill of reading independently when focusing on reading comprehension. Answer b is incorrect because although this may be helpful for students, practicing their comprehension skills is likely a better strategy. Answer c is incorrect because speech-to-text software would be more effective for students who struggle with writing.

116. C: Although it may be beneficial to allow her to pass when she is called on in front of the class, this may also cause her to be self-conscious. She might not be comfortable speaking in front of the class, but she also may not want to pass. It is important to have a conversation with students like Alison to determine what they are comfortable with and how they can be best supported. Answer A is incorrect because allowing her to skip these oral presentations might make her feel less stress about talking in front of the class. Answer B is incorrect because giving her the opportunity to collaborate with peers that she knows can help her be supported in the class. Answer D is incorrect because allowing her to sit in front of the class might make it easier to access the teacher.

117. A: Cooperative learning can be beneficial to students with all kinds of disabilities because it allows for smaller groups to work together. Rather than the teacher doing the majority of instructing, cooperative learning allows the students to work together to solve problems. Many students with disabilities may struggle to participate in large class discussions, but this gives them a different kind of opportunity to learn. Answer B is incorrect because there is likely going to be the same level of support in these classes. Answer C is incorrect because students tend to receive less direct instruction from teachers in cooperative learning classrooms. Answer D is incorrect because students may or may not make more progress on IEP goals depending on the student and the goals.

118. D: In order for objectives to be time-bound, there must be a date that the objective is to be reached. This is important for ensuring that students are making adequate progress in a timely manner. If the objectives are not bound by time, then they cannot be measured. Answer a is incorrect because the progress toward the achievement is considered the measure of the goal. Answer b is incorrect because using a reasonable amount of resources shows how achievable an objective may be. Answer c is incorrect because the use of objectives leading to a desired goal is a component of relevant or realistic objectives.

119. C: Research has found that using writing as a tool for learning academic content is helpful to normally achieving and LD students, so (c), teaching students to avoid this is not a recommendation. Based on their findings, researchers recommend (a) teaching students to set specific goals that they can attain for what they will write. They advise teachers to instruct them in strategies for planning what they will write, editing what they have written, and making indicated revisions (b). Researchers also recommend that teachers give LD students instruction in using PC word processing programs (d), which can make many aspects of writing much easier for them.

120. A: Although all of these choices can be beneficial to students with traumatic brain injuries, allowing them the use of a computer is most productive with regard to writing. The use of a computer can help alleviate some of the stress and anxiety associated with the written product. Students with traumatic brain injuries often struggle with stress and anxiety, and using a computer can help with this. Answer B is incorrect because providing review sheets would be beneficial after instruction but not likely during a writing lesson. Answer C is incorrect because reducing distractions may help with focus but not specifically with the writing process. Answer D is incorrect because although slowing the pace will help students catch up, it likely will not help them with their writing.

121. B: Norm-referenced tests can be helpful in that they compare a student's score with a random sample of other students that are of the same age. This allows the evaluator to determine areas of strength and weakness for students by comparing them to others. It is important to understand where the average score stands when interpreting assessment results in order to determine appropriate instruction or programming. Answer A is incorrect because comparing a student's score to a previous score would be considered progress monitoring. Answer C is incorrect because it is important to consider where the standard deviation is when interpreting results, but the score cannot be compared to a standard deviation. Answer D is incorrect because these assessments compare all of the students, not just those with disabilities.

122. A: One of the disadvantages to teaching students individually is that they cannot interact with their peers. It can be beneficial for students to work with their peers in order to build social skills and learn from each other. Although there are many advantages to one-on-one groups, many students learn best with other students. Answer b is incorrect because students are not accessing the general education curriculum in pull-out groups whether they are individuals or small groups. Answer c is incorrect because students also don't have access to general education teachers in any kind of special education pull-out group. Answer d is incorrect because students have access to the special education curriculum with either pull-out group type.

123. A: These all cause math difficulties (A). While they are LDs in different areas, each can lead to different types of math-related learning problems. Students who have difficulty processing language (B) can have difficulty understanding math vocabulary; solving basic addition, subtraction, multiplication, and division problems; retaining facts, such as times tables; and applying their skills and knowledge to solve math problems. Students with difficulty with visual-spatial relationships (C) can understand the mathematical facts necessary, but they have trouble setting them down on paper in an organized way. They may also have trouble understanding text in a book or writing on a blackboard related to math problems. Students with sequencing or memory deficits (D) will have trouble getting steps in the right order for solving complex problems, and find it difficult to remember facts, rules, formulas, equations, etc.

124. A: A number of researchers have found that assisted reading methods achieve significant improvements in students' reading fluency. Methods using repeated readings can be both unassisted and assisted (B). Assisted reading methods, because of the need for one-on-one instruction, have been found more workable in tutoring, but too time-intensive to be incorporated successfully in traditional classrooms (C). Reading while listening takes less time by being adapted using recordings for instruction of a group rather than individual students. It is thus more efficient than assisted reading, but it is not unrelated (D) because it was adapted from assisted reading.

125. D: In order to assess younger students who may be experiencing difficulties with development, a developmental assessment can be helpful. These assessments determine the areas of strength and weakness for students and what they need to improve upon. This allows the teacher to figure out what areas need to be focused on more and if any additional supports need to be put in place for Sally. Answer a is incorrect because IQ assessments tend to evaluate the cognitive abilities of older students. Answer b is incorrect because curriculum-based assessments are used to determine the progress a student is making on their IEP goals. Answer c is incorrect because alternate assessments are used for students who do not take the typical standardized assessments.

126. B: When writing learning objectives, it is important that they are specific to the needs of the student, measurable or quantifiable, appropriately attainable for the group of students, relevant to the current topic or lesson, and include a timeframe for the student to achieve the goal. Answers A, C, and D are incorrect because they are each missing some of these SMART components.

127. D: The 1997 version of IDEA required transition planning to begin when the student was 14 years old (C). The 2004 reauthorization of this law changed the age to 16. Some students with disabilities, such as those with autism spectrum disorders, often need extended time periods for transition planning, so many special educators still advocate beginning at age 14. Some individual states also specify age 14. The later age in the current reauthorization may reflect considerations related to developmental levels. Some students with disabilities need more time to complete secondary education. However, others will graduate at age 18 (A), so this can be too late for transition planning. (Legal rights to transition planning and services transfer from parents to students when the students turn 18.) Students with disabilities have the legal right to attend school until they graduate or reach the age of 22 (B), so transition planning must start before this.

128. A: Allowing Emma to give a slideshow presentation instead of presenting orally is the best way for her to access the same curriculum as her peers. This way, she is able to prepare and learn the same material as everyone else. Access to the curriculum involves providing opportunities for students with disabilities to learn the same material as their peers. Answer b is incorrect because if she skipped the assignment, she wouldn't gain the knowledge. Answer c is incorrect because having her aide present for her does not provide her with the opportunity to give a presentation. Answer d is incorrect because although she would still learn some of the same material as her peers, she wouldn't get a chance to present.

129. A: Using modeling software can help students to understand concepts in math and science by making them visual and concrete and enabling students to manipulate them. Playing CD-ROMs containing information and using search engines (B) to find information develop and enhance the inquiry skills of students. Utilizing email and word processing programs (C) promotes students' development of their communication skills. Inputting data to a spreadsheet program and using databases (D) helps students to improve their organizational skills.

130. A: One of the challenges of identifying students who receive English learner services for special education is deciding whether or not their needs are related to a disability. It can be difficult to distinguish between a student with a disability and a student who is new to the language. It is crucial to take all of the steps that are necessary to ensure the correct placement of these students. Answer b is incorrect because if it is determined that a student is eligible for special education services, the IEP must meet their needs. Answer c is incorrect because special education services would be beneficial in providing the student access to the general education curriculum. Answer d is incorrect because the decision is based on whether or not services are needed for special education rather than the services they already received.

Practice Test #2

1. Which of the following characteristics of culture has the greatest impact on the identification of special education students?

a. The language the student speaks
b. The content the student has learned
c. The location the student comes from
d. The religion the student practices

2. Which of the following would be the least productive method for determining how a test at the end of the unit can be used to improve instruction for the next unit?

a. Identifying which questions the student struggled with
b. Identifying which students struggled on the test
c. Identifying which kinds of questions the students asked
d. Identifying which curriculum to use

3. Which of the following research-based intervention strategies would be most appropriate for a third-grade student who is working on reading fluency?

a. Multisensory techniques
b. Metacognitive strategies
c. Text structuring
d. Explicit teaching

4. Which of the following is correct about findings related to reading disabilities in children?

a. Children with reading disabilities usually have normal speech-language development
b. Children with reading disabilities and those with writing problems are in separate groups
c. Children with reading disabilities and those with math problems are in separate groups
d. Children with reading disabilities are found to have difficulties with finger recognition

5. Which of the following best describes the purpose of the standard score when interpreting assessment data?

a. To determine how spread out the numbers are
b. To determine how far a score is from the average
c. To determine the rank of the score compared to others
d. To determine the hypothetical range of scores

6. Which of the following best describes the role of the special education teacher in the multitiered system of supports (MTSS) process?

a. To provide input on students with disabilities
b. To discuss students who may need to be evaluated
c. To provide interventions for students
d. To discuss students who exit special education

7. Developmental assessments can be useful tools in the identification of students with disabilities. Which component would MOST likely be incorporated into this kind of assessment?

a. Identifying sight words
b. Identifying letter sounds
c. Identifying math facts
d. Identifying colors

8. In general, public school students with autism spectrum disorders would be more likely to demonstrate deficits in which area?

a. In his or her attention span
b. In his or her intellectual ability
c. In his or her social skills level
d. In his or her math skills level

9. Shirley's objective is to get 90% of math problems correct on each test for eight consecutive weekly tests. On the graph below, the highest point = 90%. Based on this information, when evaluating the effectiveness of her instructional program, which is the most valid conclusion?

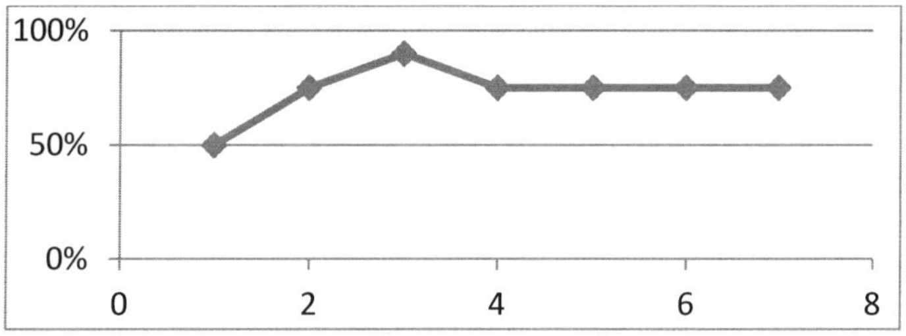

a. Shirley's program needs re-evaluation because, being stuck at 75%, she may be unable to reach 90%.
b. Shirley's program needs re-evaluation to become more challenging as she is consistently successful.
c. Shirley's program needs re-evaluation because she has reached a plateau below objective criterion.
d. Shirley's program needs no change as she has improved, is consistent, and simply needs more time.

10. When teaching an eighth-grade class, which one of the following strategies in communicating with parents best promotes a safe classroom environment?

a. Sending home the list of class rules to the parents
b. Getting to know the background and interests of the parents
c. Ensuring that behavior issues are communicated to parents
d. Reporting positive student behavior to the parents

11. Which of the following is not typically considered a service delivery model for a special education teacher?

a. Co-teaching
b. Pull-out
c. Push-in
d. Resource room

12. Which of the following is true about learned helplessness and students with disabilities?

a. Students with disabilities typically do not suffer from learned helplessness.
b. Students with disabilities often learn to control situations.
c. Students with disabilities tend to reach out for help before they get to learned helplessness.
d. Students with disabilities often feel like they have no control.

13. To ascertain a student's current achievement status in reading, math, etc., which kinds of instruments are used?

a. Cognitive test instruments
b. A sociocultural evaluation
c. Behavioral observations
d. Educational testing tools

14. From the age of 3 years to 5 years, a child's expressive vocabulary will usually:

a. Double
b. Increase by 25%
c. Increase by 50%
d. Triple

15. Which of the following functional curriculums would be most appropriate in supplementing the curriculum of a 10th-grade English class for students with autism?

a. Practice reading street signs
b. Practice reading textbooks
c. Practice reading computer terms
d. Practice reading grocery words

16. Which one of the following is the best example of a culturally responsive special education classroom?

a. Acknowledging ethnic holidays and celebrations
b. Pairing students with similar backgrounds
c. Incorporating texts from various cultures
d. Showing popular films from different cultures

17. What would be the MOST effective instructional strategy in teaching a reading lesson to students with dyslexia?

a. Using a whole-word approach
b. Using multisensory strategies
c. Using modeling
d. Using graphic organizers

18. Which of the following is the most efficient *and* effective method for teaching word recognition to a class with a variety of student levels and needs?

a. Individual direct instructions
b. Multilevel teaching practices
c. Teaching to the class median
d. Smaller groups at each level

19. In general, which is most accurate about class seating for students with learning disabilities?

a. All students with LDs should be seated in the front row of classrooms
b. Only students with visual perception or reading LDs should sit in front
c. Class seating depends on the type of LD and on the individual student
d. LDs are not sensory by nature, so seating arrangements do not matter

20. Broca's aphasia is primarily:

a. An expressive language disorder
b. A disorder of receptive language
c. A disorder of both types
d. A disorder of neither type

21. At the beginning of the week, a special education teacher asked a group of students to generate a list of verbs that make visual or sound pictures. She suggests students think of verbs that mean ways of walking, talking, eating, sitting and playing. The students spend the remainder of the week compiling the list. They notice interesting verbs as they read books, remark on less common verbs they hear in conversation or on television and locate interesting verbs in signs, magazines and other printed materials. One child begins to draw pictures to illustrate some of the verbs. Two children collaborate to create a play in which they demonstrate some of the verbs in a dance. A boy writes a song incorporating the list of verbs. The project is extremely successful. At the end of the week the students have created the following list:

TIPTOE, SCOOT, MUMBLE, MUNCH, LEAP, SPIN, DIVE, POUNCE, GLIDE, SLITHER, MOAN, WHISPER, GRUMBLE, NIBBLE, SHRILL, HOLLER, PERCH, LEAN, STOMP, MARCH, GIGGLE, HOP, STRUT, SLOUCH, GULP, HOWL, WHINE, SLURP, CROUCH, DRIBBLE, DROOL, HOOT, YELP, YOWL, GROWL, WHISTLE, SHRIEK, SNICKER, INSULT, COMPLIMENT, PLEAD, BARK, WIGGLE, TWIST, SLINK, TODDLE, TRUDGE, WANDER, STROLL.

The teacher's goal is to:

a. Enhance students' understanding of theme by encouraging them to make connections between categories of verbs.
b. Enhance students' vocabulary by encouraging them to find examples in the world around them.
c. Enhance students' understanding of context by encouraging them to explore verbs for contextual clues.
d. Enhance students' sense of curiosity by directing their attention to a number of different resources they may not have considered.

22. Which of the following best describes the implications for teaching for those who follow the behaviorist learning theory?

a. The teacher communicates through positive or negative reinforcements.
b. The teacher provides an environment that promotes self-learning.
c. The teacher facilitates collaborative learning and group work.
d. The discovery of students' behavior is guided by the teacher.

23. When working with a group of high school students on executive functioning skills, which is the best example of a summative assessment?

a. End-of-unit test
b. End-of-unit essay
c. End-of-unit presentation
d. End-of-unit performance task

24. Paul is a fourth-grade student who uses a wheelchair. Which situation would provide the greatest challenge in his ability to maneuver around the classroom?

a. Rows of desks facing the front of the classroom
b. Clusters of desks throughout the classroom
c. Desks in a circle in the middle of the classroom
d. Desks randomly spread throughout the classroom

25. Which of the following learning objectives would be considered appropriately challenging for a group of kindergarten students with math deficiencies?

a. Students will be able to add numbers.
b. Students will be able to identify numbers.
c. Students will be able to subtract numbers.
d. Students will be able to count to 100.

26. In the first week of school, a resource teacher asks her high school students to make lists of things they know how to do well. How is this activity most useful to the teacher?

a. It establishes a feeling of success in her students from the start
b. It is an informal assessment of their writing skills and gives the teacher an idea of each student's interests and abilities
c. It is a formal assessment of prior knowledge
d. It invites further discussion of each student's unique contributions and will help the class bond with mutual respect

27. Ms. Case is planning field trips in the spring for some of her high school classes. One of her groups includes Sarah, who has a diagnosis of severe autism. Which of these would be a suitable activity?

a. A trip to a local Renaissance festival
b. A nature hike to examine local flora
c. A community mixer for her age group
d. An outing to attend a rock concert

28. Which of these is a strategy that would most create a learning environment to help students with disabilities reach the goal of high school graduation?

a. Vocational training programs that satisfy the requirements for graduation
b. Coordinating education by working with teachers, parents, and administrators
c. Establishing a program to promote participation in extracurricular activities
d. Facilitating their success by setting up an alternate "pass-fail" grading plan

29. Which of the following health problems is included in the "other health impairment" disability category?

a. Asthma
b. Cerebral palsy
c. Traumatic brain injury
d. Perceptual disability

30. Gordon is a seventh-grade student with an intellectual disability. Which of the following is likely most important in ensuring that Gordon has a meaningful learning experience in the class?

a. Linking the content to real-life experiences
b. Making the content student-centered
c. Promoting self-knowledge
d. Using a variety of resources

31. Braden is a 10th-grade student with a specific learning disability. Which one of the following examples best describes when the results of his standardized testing may be unreliable?

a. If Braden did not test at the appropriate instructional level
b. If Braden did not access his accommodations
c. If Braden did not take the alternate assessment
d. If Braden did not receive proper instruction

32. Which of the following is least likely to be the responsibility of an elementary school special education teacher?

a. Communicating accommodations to general education teachers
b. Managing the schedules of paraprofessionals
c. Team-teach lessons in the classroom setting
d. Facilitation of 504 plans and meetings

33. Which of the following would be the best example of using technology to meet the needs of all kinds of learners?

a. Giving a slide show presentation
b. Grouping students to use tablets
c. Providing audiobooks to each student
d. Allowing students to use computers for independent research

34. A special education teacher assigns his students a collaborative group project. Which strategy would be most effective to benefit all students in the group?

a. Assigning one student the task of compiling and presenting the group's work
b. Allowing students to volunteer to make contributions to the project
c. Leading the activities himself and directing what the students do
d. Assigning each student an equal number of duties related to the project

35. Augmentative and Alternative Communication (AAC) devices, forearm crutches and a head pointer are assistive devices that might be used by a student with:

a. Severe intellectual disabilities.
b. Cerebral palsy.
c. Tourette syndrome.
d. Minor skeletal birth defects.

36. Javier is a third-grade student who just moved from Mexico and is struggling with the content in his English class. Which of the following is the best reason for not evaluating him for special education services right away?

a. Students who are English learners are not eligible for special education services.
b. It is best to wait and see which disability he may have.
c. It is best to wait and see the nature of his struggles.
d. New students often take a while to learn a new curriculum.

37. What statement is true regarding literacy?

a. The same literacy skills in students apply across subjects
b. The literacy demands of society have changed over time
c. Literacy required of pupils stays constant across grades
d. Literacy is best taught in the schools in a separate lesson

38. Verbal dyspraxia is:

a. Trouble with the physical act of writing
b. Refusal to speak
c. Misplacing letters within words
d. A motor skill development disorder which includes inconsistent speech errors

39. Some children have difficulty with a change in routine. The primary strategy for dealing with this problem is:

a. Maintaining the same schedule as much as possible
b. Giving advance warning of changes such as a visitor or school assembly
c. Allowing students who are likely to be upset to stay next to the teacher or a friend who can comfort them
d. Teaching relaxation techniques

40. Frank has dyslexia and is in a general education classroom. He has reading and writing sessions with his special education teacher, Ms. Miller, for one hour a day. She has taught him a number of techniques to help him decipher letters and words more easily, to distinguish between "b" and "d" in his writing, to keep his "s" going in the right direction, etc. Ms. Miller meets with Frank's general education classroom teacher, Ms. Phillips, to give her some insights and recommendations to facilitate his education. Of the following, which is NOT one of the things she might do?

a. Ask Ms. Phillips to grade Frank's papers on content but not on spelling and to excuse him from taking spelling tests.
b. Ask her to grade Frank's papers on the same basis as other students' but to highlight his reversed letters and numbers.
c. Ask her to allow Frank some additional time to complete in-class reading assignments.
d. Ask her to keep Ms. Miller informed of his progress and of areas needing more work.

41. Joseph is a 10th grader with an other health impairment due to anxiety. Which of the following would be the least effective in structuring his classroom environment?

a. Giving him a pass to leave the class when he feels anxious
b. Allowing him to take his tests in a separate setting
c. Breaking down his assignments into pieces
d. Teaching him stress-reducing activities at the beginning of each class

42. Which of the following best describes Down syndrome?

a. Gland malfunction
b. Dominant-gene transmission
c. Congenital deformity
d. Chromosomal difference

43. When screening a student for potential deficiencies as a preschooler, which of the following would be considered typical emotional development?

a. Changing the rules of a game they play
b. Being rigid with daily routines
c. Wanting to be dependent on caregivers
d. Struggling to take turns with peers

44. For students who are deaf from birth and use sign language, which of the following would an advocate of inclusion NOT consider an inclusive educational strategy?

a. Students attend a general education school and are pulled out for special instruction.
b. Students attend a regional or magnet school whose location requires living apart from their families.
c. All students and teachers in the general education school are taught to use sign language.
d. All classrooms having deaf students are assigned sign language interpreters.

45. A special education teacher feels some of his strategies aren't effective. He asks a specialist to help him improve. The specialist suggests he:

a. Begin a journal in which he considers strategies he has used. Which seemed to work? Which didn't, and why?
b. Meet with the specialist to discuss the teacher's goals.
c. Permit the specialist to drop into his classroom unannounced to observe. This will prevent the teacher from unconsciously over-preparing.
d. Set up a video camera and record several student sessions to review. They can effectively collaborate at that time.

46. How would the use of a supplementary curriculum be most appropriate for a group of high school students in a social studies class?

a. Providing the students with accommodations to access the curriculum
b. Providing the students opportunities to explore careers
c. Providing the students use of assistive technology
d. Providing the students extra credit for additional assignments

47. Which of the following is the benefit of closure when planning a lesson?

a. To ensure the students are assessed properly
b. To ensure the students understand what was learned
c. To ensure the students can demonstrate their knowledge
d. To ensure the students understand forthcoming objectives

48. Zachary is a 10th-grade student who receives special education services as a student with an other health impairment due to his ADHD, and he struggles to sit still for long periods of time. Which of the following strategies would be most effective in providing opportunities for Zachary to move around?

a. Giving Zachary a pass to move around when he needs to
b. Giving Zachary a timer to get up and stretch every 10 minutes
c. Organizing the classroom so that Zachary has his own area
d. Incorporating movement activities for the entire class

49. Educational researchers have identified three main criteria for choosing instructional media. Which of the following is NOT one of these?

a. Instructor facilitation
b. Practicality of the media
c. Student appropriateness
d. Instructional appropriateness

50. Typical cognitive development in a child between the ages of 2 and 6 would consist of which of the following?

a. A child that manipulates objects
b. A child that uses perception in their thought process
c. A child that applies logical reasoning
d. A child that has abstract thoughts

51. Mary is a 10-year-old student who has a developmental disability due to a physical impairment. Why would she not be eligible for special education services as a student with a developmental delay?

a. The developmental delay category does not include physical impairments.
b. The developmental delay category does not include students older than age 9.
c. The developmental delay category does not include students with developmental disabilities.
d. The developmental delay category does not include students younger than age 12.

52. Which statement is most likely to be true?

a. All teachers should do whatever is necessary to acquire basic knowledge of common symptoms of special needs in children, as well as typical interventions and strategies for instructing high-needs students
b. Teachers are always the most equipped individuals to determine a child's individual needs and interventions; however, most schools require evaluation by a professional
c. All children should be considered "high-needs;" teachers should teach each child as though he or she may have learning difficulties when instructing and guiding them
d. Students with learning or physiological challenges are best served in separate classrooms, where they can get the specialized attention and services they deserve

53. Which of the following conditions would not typically be associated with a student with an emotional disturbance, according to IDEA?

a. An inability to learn that cannot be explained by intellectual, sensory, or health factors
b. A disability significantly affecting verbal communication and social interaction
c. An inability to build or maintain satisfactory interpersonal relationships
d. A tendency to develop fears associated with school problems

54. Which of the following is NOT an accurate statement regarding teaching reading skills to LD students?

a. Using both visual and auditory input greatly increases comprehension
b. Using both visual and auditory input greatly increases reading speed
c. Using both visual and auditory input distracts and confuses students
d. Using both visual and auditory input works better than either alone

55. Which of the following is not an example of a strategy to improve students' generalization skills?

a. Assign field trips, role plays, etc., to apply new learning
b. Provide multiple-choice games that include analogies
c. Use a survey to identify students' favorite reinforcers
d. Use math skills in banking, loans, paying for things, etc.

56. Edgar is a seventh-grade student with an other health impairment (OHI) who is new to your caseload. Which strategy would be MOST effective in eliminating any kind of bias toward him?

a. Reviewing his Individualized Education Program (IEP) to ensure his needs are understood
b. Meeting with him to know more about his background
c. Calling his parents to introduce yourself
d. Reviewing his educational record from his previous school

57. Which of the following is true regarding individuals with developmental disabilities today?

a. Their life expectancies have not increased the way those of nondisabled people have.
b. The majority of funding for developmental disabilities is allocated for family support.
c. Mandated school services have increased expectations of support for aging at home.
d. Adults with developmental disabilities are not at higher risk for chronic health issues.

58. Which of the following classroom organization methods would be most beneficial for a teacher who includes a lot of classroom discussions?

a. Including a meeting area in the classroom
b. Arranging the desks facing toward each other
c. Having tables instead of desks
d. Ensuring that each student can move around

59. Wernicke's aphasia is primarily:

a. An expressive language disorder
b. A disorder of receptive language
c. A disorder of neither type
d. A disorder of both types

60. In teaching basic mathematics, the following actions by teachers will benefit all students. However, which one is most likely to be needed more specifically for students with special needs in a general education classroom?

a. Carefully planning the coverage and order of instructional math content
b. Judicious selection and application of the specific instructional strategies
c. Designing practice activities that take student special needs into account
d. Giving intensive, direct instruction in mathematics to individual students

61. Which is true about developmentally disabled students' transfer and maintenance of learning?

a. Instructional tasks and settings should resemble application tasks and settings.
b. Students should first acquire a skill, then gain fluency in it, and then transfer it.
c. Applying a skill should be done uniformly, without discriminating among cases.
d. Students should not practice fundamental skills until these become automatic.

62. When writing learning objectives for a lesson plan, the S in SMART stands for Specific: an objective should specify what students will achieve and in what amount. Which of the following correctly identifies one of the other initials in the SMART acronym?

a. M stands for Memorable
b. A stands for Activities
c. R stands for Resources
d. T stands for Time-based

63. Systematically evaluating and teaching social skills to students with SED is LEAST likely to involve the use of which of the following?

a. Modeling
b. Discussion
c. Extinction
d. Rehearsal

64. Which of the following is an instructional strategy that is least likely to be effective when working with a group of sixth-grade students with ADHD?

a. Offering choices to the students
b. Providing hands-on learning
c. Providing the students with a challenge
d. Repeating instructions often

Refer to the following for question 65:

Dante is a seventh-grade student who seems to have given up on schoolwork and always talks about dropping out when he is old enough. He is currently being evaluated for special education services due to his failing grades in multiple classes. His assessment results reveal that he scored in the average range on his IQ test and in the low range on his achievement test.

65. What is MOST likely the reason for his test scores?

a. Dante has a high amount of potential but has made little progress.
b. Dante has a low amount of potential but has made a lot of progress.
c. Dante has a high amount of potential and has made a lot of progress.
d. Dante has a low amount of potential and has made little progress.

Refer to the following for question 66:

A high school student struggles with applied math problems. He is given the following word math problem. He selects a. 55 hours.

A train travels from point A to point B in 3.5 hours. The same train travels from point B to point C in 2.75 hours. Another train leaves point C 1.25 hours after the first train arrives at point C. This train travels to point D in 45 minutes. The first train returns to point B in only 2.5 hours. How long does it take to travel from point A to point D?

a. 55 hours
b. 97.60 hours
c. 8.25 hours
d. 19.75 hours

66. Which of the following is the most likely explanation of the student's thought process.

a. Knows he lacks the skills to solve word problems. He arbitrarily selected the first answer without attempting to solve the problem.
b. Tried to solve the problem. He aligned all the numbers as they appeared so that 45 minutes were added with 5 in the ones column and 4 in the tens column. He also added 2.5 hours, which isn't required to solve the problem.
c. Tried to solve the problem by estimating and chose the most likely answer.
d. Selected the correct answer.

67. Which of the following is not true with regard to the role of parental participation in the IEP process?

a. Parents are members of the IEP team.
b. Parents can call an IEP meeting.
c. Parents can run an IEP meeting.
d. Parents can help develop IEP goals.

68. Which of the following pieces of information is typically not required during the pre-referral process for special education?

a. Parental consent
b. Data
c. Monitoring
d. Strategy discussion

69. Which of these social and emotional behaviors may be atypical of a third grader?

a. Complaining about friendships and others not sharing
b. Struggling to pay attention to teachers' directions
c. Having a tantrum due to a change in routine
d. Attempting to express feelings with words

70. Which of the following would be the best option in providing a fifth-grade student with a reading comprehension disability access to the curriculum in his reading class?

a. Modifying the content that the student reads
b. Accommodating the student by reading to him
c. Modifying the assignments that the student completes
d. Accommodating the student by giving him fewer questions

71. Lisa is a fifth-grade student with a disability who will often exhibit defiance in her class. Which of the following would be the best example of a formative assessment in order to evaluate Lisa's behavior?

a. Asking her to participate in class discussions
b. Conferring with her throughout the year
c. Observing her behavior in the class
d. Allowing her to skip certain lessons

72. Javier is a fourth-grade student with an emotional disturbance. Which one of the following individuals is least likely to be a member of his IEP team?

a. School psychologist
b. Director of special education
c. Student
d. School principal

73. Which of the following is the most useful skill for a learning objective in a general education setting for seventh-grade students with specific learning disabilities in the area of writing?

a. Writing sentences
b. Writing paragraphs
c. Writing essays
d. Writing words

74. Which of the following is the most accurate statement about teaching across the curriculum?

a. This is a method of planning a lesson so general that it can apply to any content area
b. Career planning for students is better addressed by other, more specific methods
c. Application of school subjects to life is best served by different methods than this
d. A single lesson plan includes math, English, reading, social studies, art, science, etc.

75. When researchers compared elementary school students with attention deficit disorder (ADD) to students with reading disabilities (RD), arithmetic disabilities (ARITHD), and normal achievers (NA) on working memory measures, they found that:

a. Students with ADD performed most comparably to students with RD
b. Students with ADD performed most similarly to students with ARITHD
c. Students with ADD performed most comparably with the NA students
d. Students with ADD performed differently from all these other groups

76. Richard is blind, has profound intellectual disabilities, and uses a wheelchair. He displays behaviors of constant head weaving and frequent hand clapping. What are some programs you might recommend for him?

a. Apply soft restraints to his head and hands to minimize or control these behaviors until he gets used to not doing them and stops.
b. Place noise-making objects like rattles, jingle bells, or tambourines in his hands to replace the clapping behavior.
c. Have the doctor examine him for a possible neurological problem that could explain the head weaving.
d. Give him a variety of sensory stimulation using sound, touch, taste, and smell, and do nothing about the head weaving.

77. What would be an example of effective feedback in a lesson plan for a third-grade class?

a. Selectively choosing students to call on
b. Immediately calling on a student after asking a question
c. Reinforcing student behavior
d. Providing corrective feedback the next day

78. Which of the following instructional media will meet all of a teacher's criteria for a specific lesson by showing motion, reproducing sounds, *and* allowing student interaction?

a. Chalkboard or easel
b. Computer software
c. Textbook/handouts
d. Overhead projector

79. Which of the following is *most* accurate about exceptional students who are gifted?

a. They typically have advanced social skills
b. Their academic performance is superior
c. Their IQ scores indicate their giftedness
d. They are often found socially immature

80. Which of these is true about frequent signs of reading problems?

a. Decoding problems with sentences/paragraphs rather than with syllables/words
b. To recognize many vocabulary words is less of a problem than to decode words
c. The ability to identify vocabulary words on sight in reading text is usually limited
d. Difficulty understanding rhymes or the order of sounds is a less common issue

81. A student with ____________ has a great deal of difficulty with the mechanical act of writing. She drops her pencil, cannot form legible letters and cannot decode what she has written.

a. A nonverbal learning disorder
b. Dyslexia
c. Dyspraxia
d. Dysgraphia

82. Brittany is a four-year-old preschool student who is administered a developmental assessment as part of her special education evaluation. Which of the following disability categories would least likely be considered as a result of these assessments?

a. Development disability
b. Speech or language impairment
c. Specific learning disability
d. Autism spectrum disorder

83. Regarding teaching strategies to improve reading fluency, teachers can encourage students to read independently by providing books with suitable difficulty levels that students find interesting. Which is true about these additional strategies?

a. Timed exercises should be avoided for creating undue pressure
b. Repetition is a very effective technique to build reading fluency
c. Readers' theatre is good for showing progress but not making it
d. Reading in pairs assists reading comprehension but not fluency

84. Which of the following best describes how daily learning objectives can be implemented to assist students who are working on adaptive skills?

a. To teach students to learn how to complete a new task
b. To teach students to improve reading ability
c. To teach students to learn about organization
d. To teach students to improve basic math skills

85. What can a teacher do in regard to the physical environment of the classroom to increase attention and learning?

a. Decorate with educational posters
b. Play music
c. Ensure the class is brightly lit
d. Arrange the desks in a circle

86. Lee's scoliosis is so severe that the OT in his residential facility had to build him a flatbed reclining wheelchair too wide to fit through the behavior specialists' office door for IQ testing. Which is the best alternative location for testing?

a. The hallway outside Lee's classroom
b. Lee's living area upstairs in the facility
c. The inner hallway outside the office
d. Inside Lee's classroom off in a corner

87. Jacob is a first-grade student who receives services as a student with autism spectrum disorders and struggles with changes in routines. What would be the best strategy to provide a supportive classroom environment?

a. The use of a visual schedule
b. Daily check-ins
c. Having the student access a paraprofessional
d. The use of a behavior plan

88. Among all persons with learning disabilities, what proportion has reading disorders?

a. 20%
b. 40%
c. 60%
d. 80%

89. Which of the following grouping techniques would likely be least effective when working with a small reading intervention group at an elementary school?

a. Grouping by ability
b. Grouping by age
c. Grouping by disability
d. Grouping by behavior

90. Christopher is a student with concerns in the area of academics who scored in the below-average range on an academic achievement test. Which of the following disability categories would Christopher most likely be eligible for?

a. Speech or language impairment
b. Other health impairment
c. Specific learning disability
d. Cognitive disability

91. What is a poor example of how to establish a positive class environment?

a. Incorporating cooperative learning activities
b. Discussing individual differences
c. Establishing consequences
d. Correcting misbehavior

92. A diabetic first grader is very pale, trembling and covered in a fine sweat. The teacher attempts to talk to the child, but the girl's response is confused and she seems highly irritable She is most likely experiencing:

a. Diabetic hypoglycemia.
b. Lack of sleep.
c. Hunger.
d. Diabetic hyperglycemia.

93. Which technique would be MOST appropriate for a student with a specific learning disability in reading to access the curriculum?

a. Modifications
b. Assistive technology
c. Accommodations
d. Adaptations

94. Of the following, which is the best example of a learning objective in a lesson plan?

a. John will demonstrate that he is able to read and comprehend at his grade level.
b. John will score at least 80% on all specified reading comprehension tests by June 1.
c. John will be able to read all grade-level materials, demonstrating 100% comprehension.
d. John will complete the assigned activity for reading and comprehending grade-level materials.

95. Which of the following would be the MOST appropriate reason to use a portfolio when assessing students with disabilities?

a. In order to determine what a student knows at the end of a unit
b. In order to determine what a student's areas of interest are
c. In order to determine how much progress a student makes
d. In order to determine how a student compares to their peers

96. How can a teacher teach spelling effectively?

a. Students who have an understanding of letter-sound association do not need to be taught to spell. If they can say a word, they can spell it.
b. Students who have an understanding of letter-sound association and can identify syllables and recognize when the base word has a Latin, Greek or Indo-European ancestry don't need to be taught to spell. They can deduce what is most likely the correct spelling using a combination of these strategies. A teacher who posts charts organizing words into their ancestor families, phonemic units and word-sound families is efficiently teaching spelling. The rest is up to the student.
c. Students who spell poorly will be at a disadvantage for the rest of their lives. It is essential students spend at least 15 minutes a day drilling spelling words until they know them forward and backward. The teacher should alternate between students individually writing a new word 25 times and the entire class chanting the words.
d. Students should be taught writing is a process. By applying spelling patterns found in word families, the spelling of many words can be deduced.

97. Which one of the following components is most important in attaining goals that are measurable?

a. Concrete evidence
b. Cost analysis
c. Clarified descriptions
d. Overarching objectives

98. Which of the following examples is least likely to be considered a formative assessment technique?

a. Analyzing student work
b. Strategic questioning
c. Unit pretests
d. Exit tickets

99. When teaching an eighth-grade geography class with multiple students that require additional support personnel inside the class, which is the best strategy in organizing the classroom?

a. Having rows of desks
b. Having desk clusters
c. Having desks in circles
d. Having long tables

100. When working as a case manager for students with Individualized Education Programs (IEPs), which role must be taken on as part of that duty?

a. Ensuring students on the caseload do not fail.
b. Ensuring students on the caseload attend class.
c. Ensuring students on the caseload meet IEP goals.
d. Ensuring students on the caseload access accommodations.

101. Which of the following is the best example of an evidence-based assessment of a student's basic writing skills?

a. Test of Written Language (TOWL)
b. Informal observation by teacher
c. A classroom writing inventory
d. A rubric-based assessment

102. Jason is a second-grade student with an intellectual disability. Which of the following characteristics would you most expect to impact his educational performance?

a. Significantly subaverage general intellectual functioning
b. Concomitant impairments that cause severe educational needs
c. Disorder in one or more of the basic psychological processes
d. An injury to the brain caused by an external force

103. Brian is a 12th-grade student with an intellectual disability. Which of the following would be the best example of a functional curriculum in his science class?

a. Learning how to conduct an experiment
b. Learning how to read a book about planets
c. Learning how to maintain a garden
d. Learning how to calculate speed

104. Joseph has Down syndrome. He can communicate with short, simple verbal phrases. He can read only a few words that he learned over a long time. He lives just a few blocks from his school. His area is not served by the school bus system. His teacher has a goal for Joseph to learn the directions to and from school so his mother will no longer need to accompany him. Which of these would be a good way for her to work with him on this goal?

a. Send Joseph out first with a map, monitoring him remotely.
b. Send Joseph out first with written directions and shadow him from a distance.
c. Walk with Joseph, prompting him to verbalize the route until he learns it.
d. Gradually decrease the number of days his mother walks with him

105. Jessica is a ninth-grade student who struggles with becoming distracted while she works in the general education setting. Which of the following methods of differentiated instruction would be most beneficial to Jessica?

a. Differentiating the learning environment
b. Differentiating the content
c. Differentiating the process
d. Differentiating the product

106. Suzie is a sixth-grade student with a specific learning disability whose parents have little or no involvement and typically do not respond when the school contacts them. Which of the following strategies would be most effective in involving them in the IEP process?

a. Continuing to reach out to them until they respond
b. Sending home forms for them to fill out
c. Offering that they participate in the meeting by phone
d. Trying to get a hold of a different family member

107. Why are objectives important for lesson planning when teaching a group of students with deficits in executive functioning?

a. To provide students the opportunity to plan what they will be learning
b. To assess students at the end of the lecture
c. To give students a task to complete during their learning
d. To keep students focused on one task

108. Kevin is an eighth grader with behavioral challenges, which makes it difficult for him to stay in the classroom. What would be the best strategy to ensure that he is able to access the general education curriculum?

a. Allowing him to complete less work than the other students
b. Having him complete his work outside of the classroom
c. Requiring that he complete only the work he does in the classroom
d. Allowing him to stay in the classroom without completing work and just listening to instruction

109. Trevor is a fifth-grade student with co-occurring conditions as a student with a specific learning disability and an emotional disturbance. Which of the following is a benefit of identifying Trevor in both of these areas?

a. Trevor can receive academic and emotional support.
b. Trevor can be placed in a self-contained classroom.
c. Trevor can have a behavior plan.
d. Trevor can be eligible for alternative placement.

110. When working with a small group of students that struggle with study skills, which instructional strategy would be the MOST effective?

a. Group discussion
b. Independent practice
c. Portfolio development
d. Cooperative learning

111. Anna is a fourth-grade student with a disability who is struggling with reading comprehension in her social studies class. Which of the following would be the best option for ensuring that Anna can appropriately access the general education curriculum?

a. Moving Anna to the third-grade social studies class
b. Reteaching the concepts in her special education class
c. Placing a paraprofessional in her social studies class
d. Modifying the content in her social studies class

112. Which of the following is true about reading?

a. Students can best learn to read through reading to learn
b. Students can learn to read and read to learn concurrently
c. Students cannot read to learn until after learning to read
d. Students in early grades will not read unless it is to learn

113. In which one of the following disability categories would you expect to identify more boys for special education services than girls?

a. Other health impairment
b. Specific learning disability
c. Intellectual disability
d. Deaf-blindness

114. Which of the following is not one of the benefits of using curriculum-based assessments?

a. To measure short-term student growth
b. To match all of the standards on the classroom curriculum
c. To inform a teacher's instruction
d. To motivate students to improve

115. The school psychologist can be a crucial member of the Individualized Education Program team. Which responsibility does the psychologist typically hold?

a. Administering IQ tests
b. Administering achievement tests
c. Administering progress monitoring probes
d. Administering transition planning inventories

116. Which of the following best describes one of the roles of the special education paraprofessional in a middle school setting?

a. Toileting students with disabilities
b. Collaborating with general education teachers
c. Communicating with parents
d. Attending IEP meetings

117. What strategy listed here is most designed to promote generalization of learning?

a. Having a student practice a new skill in a variety of different settings/contexts
b. Having a student practice a new skill regularly and periodically testing that skill
c. Having a student practice a complex skill one step at a time, then adding steps
d. Having a student practice a new skill in class before applying it in real-life tasks

118. Amy finds it problematic to take notes simultaneously while listening to her teacher. This is most associated with:

a. Visual motor coordination
b. Writing disorder/dysgraphia
c. Auditory motor coordination
d. A reading disorder or dyslexia

119. Which of the following is most applicable to providing access to the curriculum for a student who is hard of hearing?

a. Speech-to-text software
b. Text-to-speech software
c. Magnification of the text
d. Text with enlarged print

120. Which of the following best describes how an intelligence test can guide instruction?

a. To determine whether or not a student has an intellectual disability
b. To determine whether a student has an emotional disability
c. To determine which accommodations students should access
d. To determine whether a student has a learning disability

121. Which of the following models used in planning instruction for students with disabilities is described as an example of "student-directed planning"?

a. The model and process of Group Action Planning (GAP)
b. The Choosing Options and Accommodations for Children (COACH) model
c. The model and process of Making Action Plans (MAPs)
d. The Planning Alternative Tomorrows with Hope (PATH) model

122. Which of the following is the best strategy in teaching students with coexisting disabilities?

a. Teaching to each disability separately
b. Teaching the student as a whole
c. Teaching to the needs of the most impacted disability
d. Teaching to both disabilities at the same time

123. Jadon is a second-grade student with a goal in written expression. Which of the following curriculum-based assessments would be most appropriate in assessing his progress on his written expression goal?

a. Giving him 10 minutes to write as essay
b. Giving him 3 minutes to write spelling words
c. Giving him 3 minutes to write a paragraph
d. Giving him 1 minute to write a sentence

124. Which of the following is not likely to be included in both oral language achievement and written language achievement testing?

a. Mechanics
b. Narratives
c. Forming sentences
d. Both include all these

125. Which of the following intervention strategies would be most effective in assisting a student who struggles to learn vocabulary terms?

a. Providing them with a multisensory model
b. Supplying visuals with the words
c. Creating frequent vocabulary quizzes
d. Allowing students to use a dictionary

126. Shamus is an eighth-grade student with a specific learning disability in the area of written expression. Which of the following is the best example of a curriculum-based measure to monitor his progress in this area?

a. Giving him a story starter and counting his writing sequences
b. Giving him a list of spelling words to memorize and spell
c. Giving him a class period to construct an essay
d. Giving him a picture and asking him to write a sentence

127. Which of the following strategies is likely to be most effective in overcoming any kind of personal cultural biases when working with students with disabilities?

a. Learning about why the cultural bias takes place
b. Being objective when evaluating these students
c. Treating each of the students the same way
d. Encouraging cross-group participation among peers

128. What would be the MOST appropriate least restrictive environment (LRE) for a fourth-grade student with a specific learning disability in reading fluency?

a. General education classes all day
b. General education classes most of the day with a small group pullout
c. Special education classes most of the day with one general education class
d. Special education classes all day

129. When working with students on writing their name in a kindergarten class, which of the following would be the least effective in generalizing this skill?

a. Asking students to practice in the classroom during free time
b. Asking students to practice at home with their parents
c. Asking students to practice when they go to art class
d. Asking students to practice with their friends

130. Which of the following is true of the "multiple disabilities" category?

a. Deaf-blindness can be included in the multiple disabilities category.
b. Orthopedic impairments cannot be included in the multiple disabilities category.
c. Students with multiple disabilities cannot be accommodated solely for one impairment.
d. Students with multiple disabilities remain in this category throughout their schooling.

Answer Key and Explanations for Test #2

1. B: Although all of these factors can have a significant impact on a student, the content the student has learned has the greatest impact on the special education identification process. Students may come from many different cultures and have learned different topics and ideas. The special education identification process will look at a student's progress and how much they know about certain subjects compared with their peers. Answer A is incorrect because although the language a student speaks is important, it does not necessarily correspond to whether or not they should receive special education services. Answer C is incorrect because knowing where a student comes from can be helpful, but it does not impact identification. Answer D is incorrect because religion also does not impact identification.

2. D: It is likely not going to be useful to change curriculum for the next unit because of the performance of students. It will be more beneficial to take a look at some of the instructional strategies used and if there were ways to make the learning more meaningful and productive for the students being tested. This is especially the case for students with disabilities and meeting the needs of each student in the class. Answer A is incorrect because determining which kinds of questions that students struggled with can allow the teacher to redesign or modify those questions for the next test. Answer B is incorrect because identifying which students struggled allows the teacher to keep a closer eye on or accommodate some of these students. Answer C is incorrect because understanding the kinds of questions that the students asked can help to fill some of the holes that might have been left throughout the teaching.

3. A: Multisensory techniques have proven to be beneficial when teaching students who struggle with reading fluency. Many students who struggle are kinesthetic or visual learners and do better when they can see or manipulate the letter. This kind of strategy focuses on breaking down the letters in the words rather than the whole-word approach. Answer B is incorrect because metacognitive strategies include thinking strategies that would be involved with comprehension. Answer C is incorrect because text structuring involves breaking down sentences rather than letters. Answer D is incorrect because explicit teaching tends to be more productive when working on reading comprehension.

4. D: Children with reading disabilities are found (Fletcher et al) to have difficulty with differentiating among fingers. This was found to have implications for writing because fine motor skill indices such as finger tapping, finger succession, repetition, and localization were all found to relate to writing (Rutberg and Berninger). Children with reading disabilities are found more likely than those without reading disabilities to experience delays in their spoken language (A), to have difficulties with writing (B), and to have mathematics disabilities as well (C).

5. B: The standard score in an assessment is used to give the student a numbered score in order to compare that number to the average. Many tests will consider 100 to be the average standard score based on the results of the assessments. Students will then be given standard scores that are compared to that average score. Answer A is incorrect because the standard deviation typically determines how spread out the numbers are. Answer C is incorrect because comparing the rank of the score to other students is considered the percentile rank. Answer D is incorrect because the hypothetical range of scores is considered the confidence interval.

6. B: Although all of these choices may be involved in the MTSS process in some capacity, it is most likely that the special education teacher discusses which students may need to be evaluated for special education services. The MTSS process is designed to provide general education support for students who may be struggling academically, socially, or emotionally. The special education teacher is typically involved in this process to provide input on students who may not be responding appropriately to these interventions and need to be evaluated for special education services. Answer A is incorrect because the MTSS process is not typically designed to provide support for students who are already identified as having disabilities. Answer C is incorrect because the special education teacher typically is not the individual responsible for providing these general education interventions. Answer D is incorrect because although it may be possible that students who exit special education are discussed through the MTSS process, it is more often designed for students who have yet to be evaluated.

7. B: Developmental assessments tend to be used at the preschool or kindergarten level to identify students that may have a developmental disability. Identifying letter sounds would be a major component of this and an indicator of what a student can do. Answer A is incorrect because this is a skill that would likely come along a little later. Answer C is incorrect because math facts would also be worked on in a later grade. Answer D is incorrect because identifying colors does not necessarily provide academic insight into what a student is capable of doing.

8. C: Though there are individual differences, in general, students with autism spectrum disorders are more likely to display deficits in social skills, including difficulty understanding others' facial expressions, vocal tones, gestures, and other cues; difficulty initiating or participating in conversations and generally interacting with others, et cetera. Sustaining focused attention on one activity is a common feature of autism; deficits in attention span (A) are more characteristic of students with ADD or ADHD. Students with ASDs, without coexisting intellectual disabilities, are not known for deficits in intelligence (B). Students with ASDs are more likely to display deficits in verbal skills than in math skills (D).

9. C: Shirley's program should be re-evaluated because her objective criterion is 90%, but she has scored 75% for four tests in a row. It is not valid to assume she may be unable to reach 90% (A) because she already reached 90% once (point 3). While her last four scores were consistent, they cannot be considered successful (B) because they do not meet the objective criterion. It cannot be assumed she simply needs more time (D), because her scores initially improved but then fell and have not changed over four tests. Her program should be adjusted to enable her to progress to and maintain 90%.

10. C: Although all of these choices can help in making sure the classroom is a safe environment, reporting student behavior to the parents immediately can be most effective. When students misbehave, this must be communicated to the parents so further action can potentially be taken. If it is not reported home, students may continue with these poor behaviors and put other students at risk. Answer a is incorrect because simply sending home the class rules may not work for every parent and they may not always keep track of them. Answer b is incorrect because although getting to know the background of the parents might be helpful, this may not benefit the safety of the class. Answer d is incorrect because only reporting the positive behavior can help to build a safe classroom, but it is more important to report negative behavior that might be a safety concern.

11. D: Although the resource room can be a valuable environment for special education teachers to teach in, it is considered a setting rather than a service delivery model. Service delivery models indicate how the students will receive instruction rather than where the instruction will take place. It is important to consider the needs of the students before determining which kind of service model will be implemented. Answer A is incorrect because co-teaching can be beneficial when working with a general education teacher. Answer B is incorrect because pull-out groups can help students build on the skills that they struggle with. Answer C is incorrect because pushing into classrooms can help to support students who need additional assistance with the curriculum.

12. D: Students with disabilities often suffer from learned helplessness, or a condition in which they feel like they have no control. These students will often give up because they think that nothing can be done to improve their condition. This is something that impacts individuals with disabilities as they are learning about themselves and what they are able to accomplish. Answer a is incorrect because students with disabilities will often suffer from learned helplessness. Answer b is incorrect because these students with learned helplessness have a difficult time controlling situations. Answer c is incorrect because students with disabilities do not always have the chance to reach out for help before they get to learned helplessness.

13. D: Educational testing tools (d) are used to determine a student's current achievement in academic subjects. Cognitive test instruments (a) are given as part of the psychological evaluation and determine cognitive development and abilities rather than academic achievement. A sociocultural evaluation (b) is usually made by a school social worker, often by interviewing parents, to establish a developmental history and collect information about environmental influences. Behavioral observations (c) are used to gather data about a student's behaviors, often to aid in making a functional behavior analysis that may inform a behavior intervention plan, but would not determine academic achievement levels.

14. C: From the age of 3 years to 5 years, a child's spoken vocabulary will typically increase by 50% (c). A typical 3-year-old will have a maximum expressive vocabulary of around 1,000 words*; by age 5, this will have increased to around 1,500 words. (*Children develop vocabularies of around 300 to 1,000 words in their first three years; the increase percentage here is based on the high end.) Vocabulary development is more rapid from age 1 to 3 since the child is starting from nothing and has more words to learn. If the child's earlier development has been optimal, the additional increase in spoken vocabulary by age 5 is 50%, making (a), (b), and (d) incorrect.

15. D: Although all of these choices can be beneficial in helping these students with tasks they may need after high school, having knowledge of grocery words will likely help them the most. These students are likely to visit grocery stores frequently and will need to be able to read certain words in order to make purchases. Functional curriculum can help students with skills they will need when they are finished with school. Answer A is incorrect because although reading street signs can help these students, they may or may not experience driving. Answer B is incorrect because reading textbooks will likely not be a skill they will need. Answer C is incorrect because even though these students will likely use computers throughout their life, this is something that can be self-taught or practiced at home.

16. C: Although all of these strategies may be beneficial at certain times, incorporating texts from various cultures allows students to learn about other parts of the world. It is a good idea to incorporate texts from some of the backgrounds of the students in the class as a way for others to learn more about that student. It is important to make those students from backgrounds that others may not know about feel comfortable in class. Answer A is incorrect because simply recognizing holidays does not necessarily teach students about that culture. Answer B is incorrect because pairing students with similar backgrounds does not teach the other students in the class. Answer D is incorrect because films do not always portray cultures the way a book does and can misconstrue certain aspects of a culture.

17. B: Multisensory strategies, including the use of touch in manipulating letters or tapping the letters with their fingers, can be effective strategies for students with dyslexia. This sensory approach allows them to break down words and memorize them in different ways. Answer A is incorrect because the whole-word approach does not tend to be as effective for students with dyslexia. Answer C is incorrect because modeling may not be appropriate as the students need to use the strategies themselves. Answer D is incorrect because graphic organizers may be advanced for teaching reading.

18. B: Using multilevel teaching practices is an effective method to teach word recognition to a class of students with many reading levels and diverse needs. Giving direct instruction to individual students (A) is very effective but not efficient, and can be impossible for one teacher with typical class sizes. Creating smaller groups for each level (D) is similarly inefficient as the teacher could end up with too many groups to teach in the time allowed. Teaching to the median (C) leaves out too many students who are below or above the medium range that the median targets. Multilevel practices address a variety of reading levels and allow adaptations for special student needs.

19. A: In general, the most accurate statement is that (A) all students with LDs should be seated in the front row of the classroom. This does not apply only to students with visual perception or reading LDs (B). While many classroom accommodations should be tailored to the individual LD student (C), classroom seating in general should give LD students the best possible access to the teacher, blackboard, overhead projection, and other learning aids to keep from compounding their problems with perception, interpretation, integration, etc., by adding problems with access to the instruction. Although LDs are not sensory by nature (D) like impaired vision or hearing, this does not make seating irrelevant. Students can concentrate more on working around their individual LDs to learn when they do not have to concentrate harder on accessing the material.

20. A: Broca's aphasia is primarily (a) an expressive language disorder. It causes difficulty with facets of expressive language, including processes involving recall of specific words, constructing sentences with correct syntax, and other aspects of speaking and writing. It is not a disorder of receptive language (b), which affects comprehension rather than production, or of both types (c). Since (a) is correct, answer (d), neither type, is incorrect.

21. B: Enhance students' vocabulary by encouraging them to find examples in the world around them. Often children have richer vocabularies than they realize. This project simultaneously encourages students to remember words they already know and to learn other words with similar meanings.

22. A: The behaviorist learning theory states that the teacher teaches correct behaviors and the students understand them and apply them in the classroom. This theory is based on positive and negative reinforcement in order for students to learn the behaviors. This is important in understanding which techniques and learning theories might be best for certain students as they learn. Answer B is incorrect because the behaviorist theory states that the student is shaped through reinforcement rather than self-learning. Answer C is incorrect because the teacher facilitating collaborative groups is an example of the constructivist learning theory. Answer D is incorrect because the teacher guiding students in understanding the environment is an example of the cognitivism theory.

23. D: When assessing students at the end of a unit who are working on executive functioning skills, it is best to see what they are able to do. A performance task allows them to complete a task that demonstrates their knowledge of executive functioning. Answer A is incorrect because a test doesn't show that they can complete a certain task. Answer B is incorrect because an essay would not show that they can perform certain skills they may have learned. Answer C is incorrect because presenting information does not necessarily mean that they have learned to complete something on their own.

24. D: When organizing the classroom to meet the needs with accessibility concerns such as wheelchairs, it is always important to consider the path in and out of the classroom. If the desks are spread randomly throughout the class, it may be difficult for a student to maneuver in and out. Answers A, B, and C are incorrect because each of these provides organization and gives Paul and the other students an easy path.

25. B: Students with math deficiencies at the kindergarten level will likely need instruction and practice on basic concepts. Before students can begin more complex skills such as adding and subtracting, they must be able to identify numbers. A learning objective that relates to identifying numbers would be considered most appropriate for students who are struggling with math. Answer A is incorrect because adding is likely a skill that they will not have learned yet. Answer C is incorrect because subtracting numbers is a difficult skill for kindergarten students. Answer D is incorrect because counting to 100 would likely be too difficult.

26. B: It is an informal assessment of their writing and also gives the teacher an idea of each student's interests, abilities and skills. This assignment gives the teacher an idea of her students' writing abilities at the beginning of the year. She can return to this piece of writing during the school year to assess progress.

27. B: A Renaissance festival would be crowded and noisy, with many different smells, sights, and sounds. The magnitude and variety of sensory stimuli would be overwhelming to most individuals with autism. Therefore option A is incorrect.

A nature hike is likely to be in a quiet and tranquil environment. With plants as the main sensory stimuli, an autistic individual would have the opportunity to focus on examining them closely. Many autistic individuals are susceptible to sensory overload from environmental stimuli; many are also very good at focused, circumscribed activities wherein they can apply their intellectual abilities to specific tasks. Therefore option B is correct.

A community mixer is a social event. Most people with autism have difficulty with social interactions. Typically they have difficulty recognizing and interpreting social cues such as facial expressions and body language. In addition to the social emphasis, a mixer would also be noisy and crowded, which would be over-stimulating to an autistic student. Therefore option C is incorrect.

A rock concert would involve over-amplified music, which can be painful to many individuals with autism. And it would be crowded with many people. Therefore option D is incorrect.

28. B: A learning environment conducive to helping students with disabilities reach graduation can be created through ensuring that the student, parents, teachers, and school administrators are regularly involved in a collaboration to coordinate the student's education for individual needs and strengths. Vocational training (A) is not suitable to all students with disabilities. For example, many students with physical disabilities or specific learning disabilities have continued to college and graduate school and have become professionals. Promoting extracurricular participation (C) is valuable for a well-rounded student experience, but not specifically for graduation. Using "pass-fail" grading (D) contradicts the principles of inclusive education; students with disabilities may be provided with adaptations to materials and methods, including difficulty levels, to accommodate their disabilities rather than using disparate, inequitable grading systems.

29. A: One of the health problems that is included in the other health impairment category, according to the Individuals with Disabilities Education Act (IDEA), is asthma. A student with an other health impairment has limited strength, vitality, or alertness due to an acute health problem. If a student has an acute case of asthma that impacts their ability to function in the educational environment, they may be eligible for the other health impairment category. Answer b is incorrect because cerebral palsy would fall into the "orthopedic impairment" category. Answer c is incorrect because traumatic brain injury has its own category. Answer d is incorrect because a student with a perceptual disability would fall under the "specific learning disability" category.

30. A: Although all of these strategies may be helpful in creating a meaningful learning experience for Gordon, connecting the content to real-life experiences can have the most value. Students with intellectual disabilities often learn best by practicing the content they learn rather than simply hearing about it. Because of this, applying what they learn will likely be something they remember longer and can take more from. Answer b is incorrect because simply making the content student-centered may not always provide meaning to these students. Answer c is incorrect because promoting self-knowledge would likely be a better strategy for students who can explore opportunities independently. Answer d is incorrect because simply having many resources may not necessarily provide much meaning.

31. B: Although all of these factors may be taken into consideration, it is important for students to access their accommodations in order for the test to be reliable. If a student like Braden did not have the accommodations that he is entitled to receive because of the impact of his disability, the test will not be reliable. Many students with learning disabilities will have accommodations on standardized assessments such as extended time or oral presentation of the test. Answer a is incorrect because standardized tests do not necessarily align with what the students are learning in the classroom. Answer c is incorrect because the alternate assessment is designed for students who cannot access the typical standardized assessment. Answer d is incorrect because it may be difficult to determine what proper instruction looks like for specific students.

32. D: Although special education teachers have a variety of roles and responsibilities, facilitating 504 plans is typically not one of them. These plans are often administered by the school counselors or building administrators. Although it is possible that special education teachers are involved in this process in some capacity, it is typically not the expectation. Answer A is incorrect because communicating student accommodations to general education teachers is a crucial responsibility of the special education teacher. Answer B is incorrect because the special education teacher is typically responsible for assisting in developing the schedule for paraprofessionals. Answer C is incorrect because team-teaching lessons with general education teachers is also often a responsibility in ensuring the instruction is differentiated.

33. B: In order to use technology to meet the needs of all kinds of learners, it is important to allow students some freedom to learn using the method that meets their needs. When students are able to access their peers, they can learn using a variety of methods including collaboration. This allows the students to work with each other in a variety of ways while using the tablet, which may include videos, articles, and other types of projects. Answer a is incorrect because a slide show presentation likely will only target a certain group of students in the class. Answer c is incorrect because audiobooks may be beneficial to some students but not to others. Answer d is incorrect because simply giving them computers may not be productive for each student in the class to work independently.

34. D: Assigning one student to compile and present the group's work could result in that student doing more of the project than the others. This would not be truly collaborative. Therefore option A is incorrect.

Allowing students to volunteer to contribute to the project will result in some students doing most or all of the work while others end up doing little or none. This is not collaboration. Therefore option B is incorrect.

For the teacher to lead the activity and direct what the students do would not be a collaborative group project. The students should be learning to cooperate with one another and to be more independent in conducting the project. The description in this option is a traditional teacher-led activity. Therefore option C is incorrect.

Assigning each student an equal number of duties related to the project is a way to ensure that they all do equal amounts of work. The students will still be conducting the project themselves and working cooperatively together, but the teacher's initial assignment will prevent unequal distribution of participation. Therefore, option D is correct.

35. B: Cerebral palsy. Cerebral palsy is an umbrella term that groups neurological childhood disorders that affect muscular control. It does not worsen over time and the cause is located in damaged areas of the brain that control muscle movement. Depending upon the severity of the disorder, a child with cerebral palsy might benefit from an AAC device to help in speaking, forearm crutches to assist in walking or a head pointer for a child whose best motor control is his head.

36. C: Before evaluating him for special education services, it is best to see if his struggles are related to his lack of English skills or if he might have a disability. Testing him right away makes it difficult to make that determination without putting some interventions in place. It is best practice to wait and see what steps need to be taken first. Answer a is incorrect because English learners are eligible for special education services if they are determined to be eligible. Answer b is incorrect because he may or may not have a disability at all. Answer d is incorrect because although it may take him a while to learn the curriculum, this is not necessary in order to evaluate a student for special education.

37. B: Modern society demands greater literacy today than in the past. For example, as cited by Dr. Rebecca C. Faulkner, the Air Force manual for repairing fighter planes was seven pages long in World War II and 7,000 pages long in 2008. The same literacy skills in students do not apply across all subjects (A) because different literacy skills are needed for different content areas. Literacy required of school pupils also does not stay constant across grades (C) because literacy requirements advance along with each advance in grade level. Finally, literacy is not best taught in schools as a separate lesson (D) because that would be insufficient; in order to meet the changing demands of society, literacy must be taught and incorporated throughout the school day.

38. D: A motor skill development disorder which includes speech errors that don't clearly follow a pattern and so appear to be inconsistent. An example is a student who can pronounce /p/ when it is followed by a long i, as in pine, but not when followed by an ou diphthong, as in pout. Verbally dyspraxic individuals are unable to correctly place the tongue, lips and jaw for consistent sounds that can be organized into syllables. Dyspraxia appears to be a brain disorder in which the area that controls production of particular sounds is damaged.

39. A: One has to have the regular routine first, and then one can have remedial strategies for breaks in the routine. Some students, especially the youngest students, have difficulty coping with change; they need the stability of routine and find deviations from the norm to be threatening or frightening. The primary strategy for dealing with this situation is to maintain the posted schedule as much as possible. When visitors or special events do occur, it helps, of course, to prepare the students by telling them in advance of the change in schedule. Those children who are still disturbed by the change can be helped by being near someone they trust during the visit or activity. The teacher can even teach relaxation techniques to the students and suggest these techniques when a student appears to be having anxiety over a change in routine.

40. A: Asking the general education classroom teacher to excuse Frank from spelling tests and not to grade him on spelling would not be in the best interests of Frank's education. He is getting special education instruction to help him work on and overcome his learning disability. Excusing him from tasks that are harder but not impossible for him would do him a disservice. It would also set him apart from other students, who might resent him, and it would call more attention to his disability, thus making it harder for him to fit in with the general education classroom. This is something Ms. Miller should NOT do. Therefore option A is correct.

Asking Ms. Phillips to highlight Frank's reversed letters and numbers is a useful way to help him focus on his errors. He can bring his highlighted papers to Ms. Miller and they can work on these together. This is something Ms. Miller should do. Therefore option B is incorrect.

Allowing Frank additional time to complete in-class reading is not the same as excusing him from spelling tests or grades. This is a more acceptable accommodation. It can be done without calling other students' attention to it, which might provoke envy or resentment. Ms. Phillips can simply allow a slightly longer total time for in-class reading, with instructions for students to begin their comprehension questions when done reading. That way every student works at his or her own pace. This is something Ms. Miller could do. Therefore option C is incorrect.

Asking Ms. Phillips to keep Ms. Miller apprised of Frank's progress as well as any areas she would like him to work on more with Ms. Miller is a good idea. It would allow both teachers to help Frank focus on the areas in which he needs more work. This is something Ms. Miller should do. Therefore option D is incorrect.

41. D: Although teaching a student with anxiety about stress-reducing activities can be beneficial, it may not be ideal to do it at the beginning of the class period. This could potentially make the student feel overwhelmed or that they have one more thing to deal with. Students with anxiety may thrive in a structured environment, but it is important to be judicial about the strategies used. Answer A is incorrect because having a pass to leave the class can allow the student to feel comfortable knowing that they have a release. Answer B is incorrect because many students have anxiety around tests, and it can be helpful for them to take their test in a quiet environment. Answer C is incorrect because breaking down assignments into pieces can make them seem more manageable and cause less stress.

42. D: Down syndrome, which is caused by the presence of an extra chromosome, is the most frequent cause of intellectual disabilities in infancy.

43. A: One of the typical emotional developments of a preschool student is playing games with friends or others. Children of this age will often start to change the rules of a game or make up their own rules to make it more fun or interesting. Recognizing the emotions of students during these social interactions is important in determining whether or not they are developing at the expected rate. Answer b is incorrect because being rigid and not wanting to change their routine or schedule is not typical of a preschool student. Answer c is incorrect because preschool students should start to be less dependent on their caregivers. Answer d is incorrect because turn-taking is a skill that will most often develop before children enter preschool.

44. B: Attending general education schools and being pulled out for special education instruction is one inclusive solution for deaf students. Therefore option A is incorrect.

Regional and magnet schools for deaf students currently only exist in a few locations in the country, so students often have to live away from home to attend them. This would not be an example of inclusive education. Therefore option B is correct.

Teaching sign language to all students and teachers in the general education setting is another inclusive strategy. Therefore option C is incorrect.

Assigning interpreters to the classrooms for deaf students who use sign language is another inclusive strategy. Therefore option D is incorrect.

45. B: Meet with the specialist to discuss the teacher's goals. It isn't possible to determine if strategies are effective or determine a future course unless the teacher has a firm grasp of his goals and expectations.

46. B: Supplementary curriculum is typically designed to provide opportunities for students to explore experiences that they might be interested in after high school. This may look different for each student, but it can be beneficial in providing students opportunities that they may not otherwise have. A supplementary curriculum can be used for all students but is typically designed for students who may need additional support in accessing a job after high school. Answer A is incorrect because supplementary curriculum typically does not simply mean that the students can access their accommodations. Answer C is incorrect because although assistive technology can be involved in supplementary curriculum, it may not always be. Answer D is incorrect because a supplementary curriculum is not meant to create more work for the students.

47. B: It is important to have closure in a lesson so students have a firm grasp on the concepts they were expected to learn that particular day. Closure gives the students clarity if there was any confusion about what they were supposed to learn. Students with disabilities may need extra reminders, and closure can help with this. Answer a is incorrect because closure typically happens before or after the assessment as a method of recapping what was taught. Answer c is incorrect because the demonstration of knowledge is typically a task that the student completes so the teacher knows that they understood the task. Answer d is incorrect because although closure may connect to objectives that may be coming in the future, it mostly relates to the tasks completed within that day.

48. D: All students can benefit from movement activities as a method of stimulating their brain, so incorporating this strategy for all students would be the most beneficial. Although it may not always be possible each class period, finding creative ways to get Zachary up and moving with the rest of the class will make him feel less singled out. It is important to develop a plan for when these movement breaks are needed for students like Zachary and how they can be implemented for the entire class. Answer A is incorrect because Zachary may take advantage of the pass system and use it more than he really needs to. Answer B is incorrect because giving him a timer also might become a distraction to Zachary and other students around him. Answer C is incorrect because giving a student his own area might end up making him feel singled out.

49. A: Instructor facilitation is identified as a constraint on using instructional media (Dick, Carey, & Carey, 2001; Strauss and Frost, 1999; and Reiser and Dick, 1996), not a selection criterion.

Researchers (Reiser and Dick, 1996) identify practicality (B) as a criterion: The media should be available, understandable to the teacher, and efficient in terms of time and cost. Student appropriateness (C) is another criterion: Media chosen should be applicable to the targeted students' levels of development and experience. The third criterion is instructional appropriateness (D): The media should work with the teaching strategy planned; should afford efficient, effective lesson presentation; and should promote the students' attainment of the lesson's learning objectives.

50. B: A child that is between the ages of 2 and 6 will typically start to use perception in their thought process. Children at this age tend to be able to solve simple problems rather than complex, multidimensional ones. Psychologist Jean Piaget proposed that a child's intellectual development progresses through four stages. Answer A is incorrect because a child that is manipulating objects would typically be younger than 2. Answer C is incorrect because a child that applies logical reasoning will likely be older than 7. Answer D is incorrect because a child that has abstract thoughts will likely be 12 or older.

51. B: In order to be eligible for the developmental delay category, students must be age 9 or younger. There are many impairments that are included within the category, but students must be a certain age. According to IDEA, a student like Mary would likely be eligible in a different category because of her developmental disability. Answer A is incorrect because the developmental delay category does include students with physical impairments. Answer C is incorrect because students with developmental disabilities such as physical or emotional impairments would be eligible for the category if they meet the age requirements. Answer D is incorrect because students younger than age 10 are included in the category.

52. A: The field of education is constantly changing; the same is true of policies and regulations pertaining to children with special needs. Teachers are usually the first people to identify or intervene when a child is struggling in class. Every teacher should be responsible for educating him- or herself regarding possible problems that children might face. Without knowledge of symptoms, it will be impossible for a teacher to guide the student or parents effectively. The teacher may also find that previous knowledge of typical classroom strategies may benefit the child in question more quickly, and may prevent problems from getting worse.

53. B: A disability that significantly affects verbal communication and social interaction falls under the "autism spectrum disorder disability" category. An emotional disturbance is a condition with certain characteristics that occurs over a period of time and affects a child's educational performance. According to IDEA, students that display characteristics of autism will typically fall under the autism spectrum disorder category. Answer A is incorrect because students with emotional disturbances often have an inability to learn that cannot be explained by these factors. Answer C is incorrect because these students often have a difficult time building relationships. Answer D is incorrect because fears associated with school are also common for students with an emotional disturbance.

54. C: It is incorrect that using both visual and auditory input (C) distracts or confuses LD students. The information is reinforced for them when presented in both sensory modalities. Special educators find that students' reading comprehension can improve dramatically when spoken language is presented along with printed language (A). They also find that students with reading LDs, who typically read slowly and laboriously, can increase their reading speed just as dramatically when the auditory version is added to the visual (B). Therefore, it is correct that using visual and auditory input together is more effective than either sensory modality alone (D).

55. C: Using a survey to identify students' favorite reinforcers (C) is not an example of a strategy to improve generalization skills. It is an example of a strategy to improve students' motivation. Assigning field trips, role plays (A), simulations, etc., for students to apply their new learning is a good way to encourage them to use what they have learned in class to other situations; the teacher should give students feedback on their applications. Real-life situations are also excellent for generalizing learned skills. Multiple-choice games involving analogies (B) help students apply learning by showing their understanding of relationships among concepts or objects. Having students exercise their math skills in activities like loan financing, balancing accounts, and using money (D) is a good way to help them not only apply what they know to real life, but also realize some of the realistic, practical purposes and uses of their learning.

56. B: Meeting the student to get to know more about him and his background will provide more information so you have a better idea of how to meet his needs. Answer A is incorrect because simply reading his IEP will not give you as much personal information about who he is as a person. Answer C is incorrect because calling his parents might be helpful, but it is important to have a relationship with the student. Answer D is incorrect because knowing his history also will not help you with personal information.

57. C: According to research (e.g. Heller, UI Chicago, 2010), the generation that has received school services mandated by the IDEA has accordingly come to expect more support throughout life, including support for being able to grow older at home. This support is more necessary because life expectancies for the developmentally disabled have increased similarly to those for others (A). Although the majority of DD adults live with their families, only roughly 5% of funding for DD is used for family support (B). Research finds adults with DDs are more likely to develop chronic health problems (D).

58. B: For teachers who like to use a lot of discussion in their class, one strategy is to have the desks facing each other. This allows the students to communicate directly to each other and have conversations rather than the teacher doing most of the talking. This can also allow everyone in the class, including students with disabilities, feel needed and included in the group. Answer a is incorrect because most classrooms likely do not have enough space to accommodate a meeting area large enough for multiple students. Answer c is incorrect because although having tables might be helpful, it may be difficult for students to communicate with everyone in the class when they are at a table. Answer d is incorrect because although ensuring that students can move around is beneficial, it is more important that they can communicate with each other.

59. B: Wernicke's aphasia is primarily (B) a disorder or receptive language. It causes difficulties with understanding what other people are saying and with reading comprehension. It is not (a) an expressive language disorder, which causes difficulties with the processing required for speaking and writing language correctly. Individuals with Wernicke's aphasia are likely to be expressively fluent, at least initially. In the long term, their speech tends to become less logical, relevant, and appropriate due to not understanding others' verbal input and feedback, while their speech production still remains fluent. Since only (A) is correct, answers (C), neither, and (D), both types, are both incorrect.

60. D: Carefully planning what the content of the math instruction covers and the order in which it is taught (A), using their best judgment in choosing and applying appropriate teaching strategies (B), and designing practice activities with special needs students in mind (C) are all actions by teachers that will improve the involvement and progress of all students, including those with special needs. The action most likely to be needed specifically by some special needs students in the general education classroom is using more intensive direct instruction methods to teach them basic mathematics.

61. A: Educators and researchers working with DD students find similarities between tasks and settings during both instruction and application facilitate transfer. They also find the traditional three-stage hierarchy of skill acquisition, fluency, and transfer (B) is NOT as effective as supporting transfer from the beginning of instruction. Another factor facilitating transfer is the student's ability to discriminate (C) when/when NOT to apply a learned skill. Transfer and maintenance are additionally supported by practicing relevant basic skills until these become automatic (D): students must be fluent in foundations to attain higher learning levels.

62. D: Time stands for Time-based, i.e., the objective should specify in what length of time, or by what point in time, it is to be attained. M stands not for Memorable (A), but Measurable: the objective must be something that can be objectively measured or quantified. A stands not for Activities (B), but Appropriate: the objective should be suitable to the purpose the activity is intended to accomplish. R stands not for Resources (C), but Realistic: the objective should be possible to achieve with the instructional experience and resources available.

63. C: Extinction (C) is least likely to be used to evaluate or teach positive social skills to SED students. Extinction is a behavioral technique that involves ignoring a behavior that is reinforced when the student receives attention for engaging in that behavior. When the motivation for repeating a behavior is attention, the behavior will eventually cease due to the continued absence of this reinforcement. Modeling (A) provides students with examples of positive social behaviors which they can learn by imitating them. Discussion (B) helps students understand social interactions by getting feedback on their own and others' behavior. They can then change their social behaviors in response to the insights they gain. Rehearsal (D) allows students to practice new behaviors in a safe environment, giving them a better chance of behaving appropriately in real life situations. These techniques are often used to teach social skills.

64. C: Although each student may respond differently to challenging tasks, many students with ADHD will shut down if a task becomes too difficult. It is important to understand and recognize what the student is able to accomplish before challenging them. It can be embarrassing or cause anxiety for students who are unable to fulfill the challenge of the teacher. Answer a is incorrect because offering choices to the students allows them to feel like they are a part of the decision making. Answer b is incorrect because hands-on learning activities allow students to get up and move around. Answer d is incorrect because repeating the instructions often ensures that each student hears what is expected and does not forget.

65. A: Typically, IQ tests show what a student's potential outcomes for academic achievement can be, whereas an achievement test shows how much progress a student has made and what he or she is currently capable of doing. Answer B is incorrect because low potential would mean he had a lower IQ score. Answer C is incorrect because a lot of progress would mean that he had a higher achievement score. Answer D is incorrect because low potential would mean lower IQ scores.

66. B: Tried to solve the problem. He aligned all the numbers as they appeared so that 45 minutes were added with 5 in the ones column and 4 in the tens column. He also added 2.5 hours, which isn't required to solve the problem.

67. C: Although parents have many rights with regard to their child's IEP, running the IEP is not one of those rights. Typically, the IEP meeting will be run by a special education teacher or administrator. Parents are encouraged to be highly involved in the IEP meeting, but they are not responsible for facilitating the meeting. Answer a is incorrect because parents are important members of the IEP team. Answer b is incorrect because parents can call an IEP meeting if they believe their child's needs must be addressed. Answer d is incorrect because parents can help to develop IEP goals.

68. A: During the pre-referral process, parents are not typically required to give their consent. This process typically consists of identifying areas in which the student struggles and developing strategies to assist this student. This may consist of interventions inside or outside of the classroom in addition to accommodations or modifications. Answer b is incorrect because it is important to collect data to determine whether or not a student is making sufficient progress. Answer c is incorrect because monitoring is important because it determines whether or not new strategies need to be implemented to better meet student needs. Answer d is incorrect because constantly evaluating the strategies and discussing them as a team is a necessary component of the pre-referral process in meeting student needs.

69. C: Although tantrums are expected of younger children, a tantrum isn't typical in a third grader. Typical development in third graders includes complaining or telling on their peers, so answer A is incorrect. It is also typical for a third grader to struggle to pay attention, so answer B is incorrect. Attempting to express feelings with words is typical for a third-grade student, so answer D is incorrect.

70. B: One of the best ways to provide access to a student with a disability in the area of reading comprehension is to provide accommodations. Reading the text to the student allows them to take in what they are reading and process it more clearly than they might if reading independently. Typically, it would not be as beneficial to modify or change the expectations of what the student completes. Answer a is incorrect because modifying what the student reads does not allow them to access the curriculum that their peers are accessing. Answer c is incorrect because modifying the assignment may not give the student a chance to learn all of the material. Answer d is incorrect because giving a student fewer questions does not give them access to all of the curriculum.

71. C: Although all of these choices might be beneficial to some students in improving behavior, observing her regularly can help evaluate her behavior. If a student like Lisa is evaluated regularly, the causes of her behavior can be analyzed in order to guide instruction. It is important to constantly be thinking of new instructional practices and methods to support students with behavior struggles like Lisa. Answer a is incorrect because asking her to participate in class discussions might bring out more of the negative behavior that she tends to exhibit. Answer b is incorrect because although conferring with her might be beneficial in the short term, it is likely that her defiance will continue to arise unless the instruction changes. Answer d is incorrect because this would not be considered an assessment method but rather an instructional practice.

72. C: Students in elementary school do not typically attend their IEP meetings. These students are often too young to attend and understand the discussion at the meeting, so they are most often not invited to the meeting. It is important to understand a student's maturity level before inviting him or her to an important meeting to discuss their IEP. Answer a is incorrect because the school psychologist can be an important member of the IEP team for students with emotional disturbances in writing behavior plans or monitoring goals. Answer b is incorrect because the director of special education is also often invited to these IEP meetings. Answer d is incorrect because most school districts require a building administrator to attend IEP meetings as well.

73. B: Students in seventh grade with specific learning disabilities in the area of writing would be expected to be able to write a paragraph. Some students may have more skills than others, but most students would be able to write a paragraph. This objective may need to be modified for certain students with more severe struggles, but a student with a specific learning disability that is appropriately placed would be expected to keep up with the curriculum. Answer a is incorrect because writing sentences would likely be a skill that students would have already mastered by this age. Answer C is incorrect because being able to write an essay likely would not be expected of seventh-grade students. Answer D is incorrect because simply writing words is a skill that these students already know.

74. D: In teaching across the curriculum, one lesson plan actually incorporates all subjects taught rather than being so generic as to apply to any subject (A). For example, a spreadsheet that uses visually beautiful graphic design incorporates math and art. Teaching across the curriculum does facilitate career planning (B) because it shows students different ways that subjects learned in school apply to real life (C), including job choices.

75. C: Researchers found that when comparing working memory in students with ADD to that in students with RDs, with ARITHD, and in NA students, the attention-deficit students (c) performed most like the normal achievers tested. They thus concluded that working memory may not depend significantly on attentional factors. ADD students did not compare most to RD students (a), who demonstrated general deficits in working memory affecting both linguistic and numerical tasks. ADD students did not perform most like students with ARITHD (b), who evidenced specific numerical deficits in working memory but not linguistic ones. Because (c) is correct, answer (d), that ADD students performed differently from all these other groups, is incorrect.

76. D: Restraints should not be used except in extreme cases, to prevent injury to oneself or others. Richard's behaviors do not harm anybody. Research shows that restraining movements does not eventually stop them. Therefore, option A is incorrect.

Noise-making instruments would provide auditory stimuli for Richard but would be disruptive to others. Though his hand clapping could be a repetitive behavior due to his intellectual disabilities level, it could also be an attempt at auditory and tactile sensory self-stimulation. Therefore, option B is incorrect.

Head weaving is common in blind individuals. It is often a means of getting sensory feedback in the absence of visual stimuli and can also provide proprioceptive and kinesthetic orientation. Regardless, Richard will have a neurological assessment as part of his physician's examination, but there is no special indication to look for problems on account of head weaving. This behavior can be normal in some blind individuals. Therefore, option C is incorrect.

Because he is blind and has profound intellectual disabilities, a program of sensory stimulation using his other senses would benefit Richard as it would enrich his environment and enhance his learning ability. A need for additional sensory stimulation may also be indicated by Richard's hand clapping. Therefore, option D is correct.

77. C: One of the characteristics of an effective lesson plan is positive feedback. Reinforcing student behavior is one of the most effective ways to praise students and provide this positive feedback. Answer A is incorrect because selectively calling on students may create an imbalance of who gets called on. Answer B is incorrect because it is best to give students some time to think before asking a question. Answer D is incorrect because feedback should be provided immediately so they can make corrections.

78. B: Computer software meets all of the listed criteria. A chalkboard or easel (A) allows student interaction but does not meet the other requirements. Textbooks and handouts (C) do not fulfill any of the criteria, though they have many other desirable characteristics (portability, allowing highlighting/writing/drawing in or on them, availability after the lesson, independent use, etc.). Overhead projector (D) presentations (and slide shows or other computer presentations) allow writing/highlighting/drawing, let students control the pace, are easily modified, etc., but they do not meet these other specific criteria either.

79. D: Some gifted students excel in all areas, including athletics and social skills (A), but not necessarily. Gifted children can have different abilities and interests than peers, making social interaction awkward. They may have difficulty relating to peers with more typical abilities and interests, resulting in peers who may not want to interact with them for being different. Some gifted children prefer academic/creative activities over social activities. Some gifted children show superior academic performance (B), while some do not. Some are bored by traditional curricula (including special education for the gifted) and lack motivation, while some use unconventional methods. As a child, Albert Einstein reportedly was failed in math by a teacher for achieving correct answers without following prescribed steps. Not all gifted children get high IQ scores (C) because giftedness also includes creativity, not just intelligence. Some gifted children do not respond to standardized measures because they may think differently and/or be uninterested in test items.

80. C: Students with reading problems frequently have trouble recognizing very many vocabulary words on sight in reading text. They also often have problems decoding (sounding out) syllables and single words (A). Sight word vocabulary and word decoding are both common difficulties; one is not less of a problem than the other (B). Another common issue is trouble understanding rhyming words and/or phonemic sequencing (D).

81. D: Dysgraphia. Dysgraphic individuals cannot manage the physical act of writing. While many dysgraphics are highly intelligent and able to express themselves cogently, they have extreme difficulty holding a writing implement and shaping letters.

82. C: Developmental delays typically do not include tests that would determine a student eligible for a specific learning disability. Although these developmental assessments are beneficial in determining what a student may struggle with, it is difficult to determine the academic skills of children at such a young age. Specific learning disabilities typically manifest as students have had more instruction in reading, writing, and math. Answer A is incorrect because the developmental disability category is common for preschool students who are struggling in certain developmental areas. Answer B is incorrect because speech or language impairments are also common with preschool students. Answer D is incorrect because students with a diagnosis of autism are often identified in the autism spectrum disorder category as a preschooler.

83. B: The only true choice is (B): Repetition is very effective for building reading fluency. The teacher can have the student read a passage aloud repeatedly until s/he achieves the desired fluency, and then progress to a harder selection. Timing this exercise also promotes fluency, which includes speed as well as accuracy; therefore (A) is incorrect: Timed exercises should not be avoided in remediating fluency problems. Teachers can also use timing by giving students "speed drills" for individual words. A non-timed exercise can be having a student repeatedly read a familiar book out loud, giving feedback and direction as needed. Another technique is a readers' theatre; it is not true that this is good for showing progress but not making progress (C). The practice and feedback component of this exercise aids with improvement, even as it showcases progress in fluency. It is not true that reading in pairs increases comprehension but not fluency (D); partner/paired reading promotes both.

84. A: Adaptive skills are skills that people use every day in order to function at home, school, or work. There are many skills in caring for oneself and accessing the community that are important to practice and complete in order to demonstrate understanding. When teaching these skills, it is important to provide opportunities to practice these tasks to determine what students have mastered and what skills needs additional work. Answer b is incorrect because although improving reading ability is important, this would likely not be considered an adaptive skill. Answer c is incorrect because learning about organization is not typically a skill that is practiced in isolation when considering adaptive skills. Answer d is incorrect because basic math skills are also not considered an adaptive skill.

85. C: The physical environment of a classroom is very important to effective learning. Classrooms that are bare will promote a cold, institutional feeling. This may inhibit learning. On the other hand, classrooms cluttered with information and posters may be too overwhelming for students and thus be counterproductive. In addition to ensuring that posters with appropriate content and an appropriate amount of information are used to decorate a room, proper lighting is also essential for creating an effective learning environment. Adequate lighting should be used to maintain attention and to prevent a dark environment where students and the teacher become sleepy during the day. This is especially important after lunch. If a classroom does not have enough lighting, the teacher can use lamps to increase the brightness of a room.

86. C: The best alternative would be (c) the inner hallway outside the behavior specialists' office. Being an inner hallway, it is likely to be quieter. During class hours, most professionals' offices in this hall are empty as their occupants are doing training or monitoring in classrooms, making rounds, etc. In contrast, the hallway outside the classroom (a) is likely to be noisy during class times, with more traffic and less privacy. Lee's living area upstairs (b) is farther away, requiring more transport time, and the behavior specialists would also have to bring all their testing materials, whereas these are much more accessible in their office when they are right outside of it. Inside the classroom, even off in a corner (d), is not a good location as the class activities can distract Lee from testing, and testing can disrupt the classroom activities and distract the students and teacher as well as violating the student's privacy and confidentiality.

87. A: Visual schedules can provide students who struggle with routines support in understanding what the expectations are and will be. Seeing what the expectations are help eliminate negative behavior and promote and safe and supportive classrooms. Although daily check-ins, using a paraprofessional, and behavior plans can all be beneficial, the best support for a student who struggles with routines is a visual schedule.

88. D: Eighty percent (D) of all people with learning disabilities have reading disorders, making this the most common of the learning disabilities. Twenty percent (A) is only one-fourth the actual proportion of reading disorders among learning disabilities. Forty percent (B) is one-half the actual percentage, while 60% (C) is three-fourths of the true figure.

89. C: Although all of these grouping patterns have their own strengths and weaknesses, it makes the least sense to group students based on their disability. It is important to take into consideration many aspects including disability, but this is unlikely to be the determining factor. It is more important that the students in the group are a good match for the instruction and each other than what their disability might be. Answer A is incorrect because grouping students by ability can be effective in ensuring that the students learn at a similar pace. Answer B is incorrect because grouping by age can help ensure the students are learning the same content in class. Answer D is incorrect because grouping students by behavior can help make sure that students work well with each other.

90. C: Students who score in the below-average range on achievement tests with no other concerns will typically fall under the "specific learning disability" category. Students with specific learning disabilities have deficits in the areas of reading, writing, and math. It is important to understand the results of assessments in order to appropriately place students and provide services that the student will need. Answer a is incorrect because students with trouble in speech or communication would take a test specific to those needs. Answer b is incorrect because students who receive services under the other health impairment category will have a health impairment that impacts their access to education. Answer d is incorrect because a cognitive disability is not one of the disability categories under IDEA.

91. B: To create a positive class environment, it is important that everyone in the class feels welcome, safe, and wanted. Discussing individual differences may exclude students or make them feel uncomfortable, which would not establish a positive environment for that student. Answer A is incorrect because cooperative learning activities are a great way to establish a positive environment by having students interact. Answers C and D are incorrect because it is important to set ground rules so students understand the expectations.

92. A: Diabetic hypoglycemia. Diabetic hypoglycemia, also known as insulin reaction, occurs when blood sugar falls to a very low level. It is important to treat it quickly or the diabetic could faint, in which case an injection of glucagon is administered.

93. C: A student with a specific learning disability in reading would likely use accommodations to access the curriculum. Accommodations allow the students to access the same content as their peers with a change in presentation, timing, setting, scheduling, or formatting. This may include oral presentation of the text or extended time to read assignments. Answers A and D are incorrect because modifications and adaptations adjust the assignment and change what a student is taught. Assistive technology may be helpful in helping some students access the curriculum, but a student with a learning disability wouldn't typically access this.

94. B: This objective specifies what John should be able to do through the lesson; it is measurable by specifying a minimum score on all appropriate assessments indicated in the lesson plan; and it specifies by what time he should have achieved this. (A) does not specify how to measure or assess John's reading ability or comprehension, or any time frame. (C) not only fails to specify these things, but moreover is unrealistic in dictating 100%. (D) not only fails to specify measurability; it moreover states only what activity John will complete, but not what he should learn and be able to do through completing it.

95. C: Portfolios can be a beneficial assessment tool in many ways including accessing how much progress a student has made over a period of time. This can include a collection of writing samples, probes, or any other activity that can be measured. This can often be a more accurate measure of student growth for students with disabilities that struggle with traditional exams. Answer a is incorrect because determining what a student knows at the end of a unit would be a formative assessment. Answer b is incorrect because determining a student's interests would be an interest inventory rather than a portfolio. Answer d is incorrect because comparing a student to their peers would be considered a norm-referenced assessment.

96. D: Students should be taught that writing is a process. By applying spelling patterns found in word families, the spelling of many words can be deduced.

97. A: In order to attain a measurable goal, there must be concrete evidence that the goal is or is not being met. Without this evidence, it is difficult to determine how much progress is being made in the goal and how much is left to accomplish. Goals that are measurable are crucial to refining exactly what it is that the goal is trying to achieve. Answer b is incorrect because a cost analysis is a component of an attainable goal. Answer c is incorrect because a clarified description may be beneficial for whether or not a goal is measurable but is more closely related to the specificity of the goal. Answer d is incorrect because overarching objectives are components of relevant goals.

98. C: Unit pretests would typically be considered an example of a diagnostic assessment rather than a formative assessment. Formative assessments are designed to assess students as the learning is occurring, rather than before or after. It is important to informally assess the students while learning occurs in order to determine if the instruction needs to be adjusted. Answer a is incorrect because analyzing student work is a beneficial formative assessment in discovering what the students are capable of. Answer b is incorrect because questioning the students as the learning takes place gives the teacher an understanding of what the students know. Answer d is incorrect because exit tickets can allow the students to demonstrate what they have learned and what they still struggle with at the end of a lesson.

99. A: A classroom with rows of desks allows the support personnel to move up and down the aisles to support students. This way, they are able to easily access each one of the students. It is important that students that require support have access to that support person, who can help them if needed. Answer b is incorrect because having clusters of desks may make it difficult to access individual students. Answer c is incorrect because having desks in circles may also make it difficult to work with students. Answer d is incorrect because having long tables also limits this access.

100. D: It is the responsibility of the special education case manager to ensure that each student on his or her caseload is accessing accommodations and that general education teachers know how to implement them. Answer A is incorrect because it is not the responsibility of the case manager to make sure students do not fail. Answer B is incorrect because it is also not the responsibility of the case manager to make sure students are attending school. Answer C is incorrect because although the case manager will track the progress of students on their IEP goals, it is not their job to make sure they meet the goal.

101. A: The TOWL is an evidence-based assessment of a student's basic writing skills because its results are norm-referenced and supported by experimental research results. The other choices are all equally effective methods of assessing basic student writing. However, "evidence-based" is less descriptive of these because they rely on individual teacher methods and/or individual student writing samples, but they are not proven by evidence from research studies and do not compare student results to those of normative student sample groups.

102. A: A student with an intellectual disability will have a significantly subaverage general intellectual functioning. This will typically be combined with deficits in adaptive behavior and will be manifested during the developmental period. This is something that likely would be noticed in Jason starting from an early age. Answer B is incorrect because a concomitant, or accompanying, disability would fall under the category of multiple disabilities. Answer C is incorrect because a disorder in basic psychological processes would fall under a specific learning disability. Answer D is incorrect because an injury to the brain by an outside force would be in the "traumatic brain injury" category.

103. C: Although all of these choices relate to science and can be functional for certain students, learning how to maintain a garden is likely most appropriate for students like Brian. A functional curriculum is designed to provide opportunities for students to work on their independent living skills. Maintaining a garden is a valuable skill that can be helpful for students like Brian to learn and apply once they graduate high school. Answer a is incorrect because although conducting an experiment may be a useful skill to have, it may not be as useful as having a garden. Answer b is incorrect because learning about planets also likely is not as useful as maintaining a garden. Answer d is incorrect because calculating speed may or may not be something that students like Brian need to know after high school.

104. C: Since Joseph has never walked the route alone, he would get lost if sent out on his own now. Therefore option A is incorrect.

Sending Joseph out with written directions is not a good idea since he does not have good reading skills. And he would get lost if he went out alone without prior practice in finding his way. A teacher shadowing him would have to catch up with him to redirect him when he went the wrong way or stopped when he did not know which way to go. Therefore option B is incorrect.

Since Joseph is used to walking the route with his mother, it would be better to accompany him at first. Doing so would provide a point from which to transition gradually to his walking alone. Unlike his mother, the teacher will be prompting him to verbalize the route. Since his expressive language skills are better than his reading skills, this is a more effective modality to help him learn the directions. Therefore option C is correct.

Gradually decreasing the days his mother goes with him, e.g., having her go four days and having him go alone one day, then having her go three days and having him go alone two days, etc., is not a good idea. Joseph's mother has never taught him the route, so he does not know the directions and cannot find his way independently. Since he has always relied on his mother, he would get lost the first time he tried to go on his own. Therefore option D is incorrect.

105. A: In order for a student like Jessica to succeed in the general education setting, it is likely best to differentiate the learning environment. One way to do this would be to create a space in the classroom where there are no distractions. This way, Jessica can still access the content of her peers while still being free from distractions that might impact her ability to learn. Answer B is incorrect because differentiating the content would not be appropriate because she can still learn what the other students learn. Answer C is incorrect because differentiating the process would not be appropriate because she can still learn the content in the same way that the other students learn. Answer D is incorrect because differentiating the product would not be appropriate because she can be assessed using the same methods as other students.

106. C: Although some parents are difficult to contact and do not wish to be involved with their child's education, providing alternatives might be the best option. It is important to accommodate the needs of the parents whenever possible in an attempt to get them more involved. The input of the parents is very valuable at IEP meetings, so if having them participate by phone is the best option for them, then that should be explored. Answer A is incorrect because they are unlikely to respond if they continue to receive phone calls nonstop. Answer B is incorrect because although sending forms home may work for some parents, some kind of verbal communication would likely be more productive. Answer D is incorrect because it is important to have input from the family members that live with the student.

107. D: Students with executive functioning deficits often struggle to organize their thoughts or stay on task. Providing them with daily objectives allows them the opportunity to understand what is expected of them and to remain on task. It is important to continually review the objectives throughout the lesson so that students are reminded of what is expected. Answer a is incorrect because planning can be a difficult skill for students with executive functioning deficits. Answer b is incorrect because objectives typically are not designed as an assessment method. Answer c is incorrect because giving the student a task while they are learning is often difficult for those with executive functioning deficits.

108. A: Although each student is different and may require different levels of support, modifying the curriculum to allow the student to complete less work still allows the student to access the curriculum. Answer B is incorrect because completing work outside of the classroom does not allow him access to the teacher for instruction. Answers C and D are incorrect because just being in the classroom and not completing work does not allow a student to demonstrate knowledge of the curriculum.

109. A: Students are eligible to receive support for each one of the disability categories that they are identified in. Because of this, Trevor can receive academic support as a student with a specific learning disability and emotional support as a student with an emotional disturbance. Although students do not necessarily need to be identified as having more than one eligibility category to receive these supports, the identification of each one of these makes the services mandatory. Answer b is incorrect because Trevor would not automatically be eligible for a self-contained classroom. Answer c is incorrect because Trevor can have a behavior plan without being identified with co-occurring conditions. Answer d is incorrect because alternative placement is not determined based on co-occurring conditions.

110. A: When teaching students about study skills and how to use them, it is important to assist them in developing some methods that will work for them. Answer B is incorrect because independent practice would be difficult for students who are struggling to come up with ideas. Answer C is incorrect because developing a portfolio likely would be too much of a task to take on. Answer D is incorrect because although it may be beneficial, having the whole-group discussion is likely more valuable with the teacher's input.

111. D: Although all of these choices can be beneficial in ensuring that Anna still has access to the general education curriculum in her social studies class, modifying the content can help the most with her reading comprehension struggles. Modifying the content to include less reading or fewer questions she has to answer still allows her to learn most, if not all of what her peers learn. It is important to understand how to provide support in a way that students can still learn what their general education peers are learning whenever possible. Answer A is incorrect because it may alienate Anna to move her down a grade level. Answer B is incorrect because although reteaching concepts may be beneficial, her time with the special education teacher's time may be better spent working on her reading comprehension abilities. Answer C is incorrect because a paraprofessional likely would not be as beneficial as modifying the curriculum.

112. C: Students typically learn to read through third grade and transition to reading to learn and reading for pleasure around fourth grade. While they are learning the basics, all of their attention is focused on decoding, word recognition, vocabulary, comprehension, etc., so they cannot yet move beyond these tasks to focus on subject content. Therefore they cannot best learn to read through reading to learn (A) and they cannot do both things at the same time (B). In the early grades, students are learning reading itself and will only read for this reason, rather than only reading to learn (D).

113. A: The other health impairment category tends to identify the majority of students due to a diagnosis of attention-deficit/hyperactivity disorder (ADHD). Although boys may be identified for services more than girls in the majority of categories, it is overwhelmingly more so in the other health impairment category. According to the Centers for Disease Control and Prevention, boys are three times more likely to have ADHD than girls. Answer B is incorrect because the number of boys and girls with a specific learning disability tends to be fairly even. Answer C is incorrect because intellectual disabilities also do not have as large of a disparity as the other health impairment category. Answer D is incorrect because there is no correlation between gender and deaf-blindness.

114. B: Although there are many benefits to using curriculum-based assessments (CBAs), they do not always correlate perfectly to the classroom curriculum. Curriculum-based assessments are designed to monitor the progress of student understanding throughout instructional units to help quickly adjust instruction to meet student needs. CBAs are commonly used in conjunction with IEPs as a means of ensuring students with learning disabilities are making progress toward their particular goals. CBAs do not comprehensively measure curriculum mastery, but only serve as samples of student comprehension. Answer A is incorrect because curriculum-based assessments can measure the progress of students over a short period of time such as one week. Answer C is incorrect because a teacher's instruction can be informed based on the needs of the student and what they may need to work on. Answer D is incorrect because students can chart their scores and work toward improving them.

115. A: School psychologists are trained to administer IQ tests to students. Although it is possible for the special education teacher to assist in this process, IQ tests are typically administered by the psychologist. Answer B is incorrect because achievement tests are most often administered by the special education teacher. Answer C is incorrect because progress monitoring is completed by the special education case manager. Answer D is incorrect because transition planning inventories are also administered by the special education teacher.

116. A: One of the responsibilities of paraprofessionals in many schools is to toilet students with disabilities. This will typically involve students with severe needs who are unable to toilet themselves and need additional support in this area. Although this may not always be a requirement for every paraprofessional, it is often expected as a part of the fulfillment of the duties of the job. Answer B is incorrect because it is the responsibility of the special education teacher to collaborate with the general education teachers. Answer C is incorrect because communicating with parents should also be done by the special education teacher. Answer D is incorrect because paraprofessionals are not typically involved in IEP meetings.

117. A: Generalization of learning is the ability to apply learning across multiple and varied contexts or settings. Regular practice and periodic testing (B) are designed to promote maintenance rather than generalization. Learning one step at a time (C) is a characteristic of task analysis, which breaks complex skills or tasks down into more achievable steps and is related to promoting skill acquisition rather than generalization. Practicing a new skill before applying it to real-life situations (D) is a way to promote both acquisition and maintenance of the skill before its application and generalization.

118. C: Problems with taking notes while listening is most associated with (c) auditory motor coordination. Auditory motor coordination also allows us to follow spoken instructions. Writing down what one is listening to relies on this ability. Visual motor coordination (a) is more related to the ability to copy printed or written information. It also relates to writing itself, though not specifically writing what one is hearing, as well as typing or cutting out patterns, which all require coordinating manual motor activities with vision rather than audition (hearing). A writing disorder, or dysgraphia (b), is likely to interfere with writing complete sentences that are grammatically correct. (If neural networks for hand movement and/or immediate memory are affected, a writing disorder can also affect note-taking, but deficits in vocabulary and grammar have less impact on taking lecture notes than on original writing.) A reading disorder or dyslexia (d) affects reading, not writing.

119. A: Speech-to-text software can convert the teacher's spoken lessons, lectures, and directions to a format the students who are hard of hearing can read visually. Text-to-speech software (B), text magnification (C), and large print (D) are all more suited to providing access to the curriculum for a student who has visual disabilities.

120. C: Although there are many uses for intelligence tests, determining which accommodations a student accesses can help guide instruction. Intelligence testing is important in determining the intellectual abilities of students. These results can reveal how accommodations may benefit them in the classroom and which ones would be the most appropriate for them to access. Answer A is incorrect because although an intelligence test can be helpful in determining whether or not a student has an intellectual disability, this does not guide instruction. Answer B is incorrect because determining whether a student has an emotional disability would likely encompass more than just an intelligence test. Answer D is incorrect because learning disabilities are typically discovered through additional assessments as well.

121. B: The COACH model (Giangreco, Cloninger and Iverson, 1998) is a collaborative approach described by educational researchers as "student-directed planning," which they claim goes "beyond person-centered planning" (Wehmeyer et al, 2002) by making the student central in the process. Person-centered planning typically centers more on family and social support systems. GAP (Turnbull & Turnbull, 2002) (A); MAPs (Pearpoint, Forest, & O'Brien, 1996) (C); and PATH (D), which extends the MAPs process to develop "a more definitive plan of action," are all examples of person-centered planning.

122. B: When teaching students with coexisting disabilities, it is important to look at the student as a whole rather than someone with more than one disability. It is difficult to meet each and every need of the student if they are looked at separately. It is important to look at the student as a whole and discover how their needs can be met. Answer a is incorrect because it may be difficult to separate the disabilities in the individual student. Answer c is incorrect because although it is important to teach to the most impacted disability, there may be other needs as well. Answer d is incorrect because it could be difficult to teach to multiple disabilities at once.

123. C: The most appropriate probe for a curriculum-based assessment in the area of written expression for a second grader would be to write a paragraph. Curriculum-based assessments are designed to see what a child is able to do by challenging them but giving them something that can be accomplished at a certain point. Writing paragraphs is something that students in second grade are likely working on or striving toward, which is why this probe would be beneficial for Jadon. Answer A is incorrect because second graders likely do not know how to write an essay yet. Answer B is incorrect because although spelling may be helpful, being able to compose sentences tends to be more valuable. Answer D is incorrect because writing one sentence likely does not provide quite enough information.

124. A: Mechanics (A) are likely to be included in written language achievement testing, but not in oral language achievement testing. Spelling and punctuation cannot be assessed in speech, and other mechanics are never as correct in speech as in writing, even by those without any learning disabilities. Narratives (B) are likely to be included in both types of testing as they demonstrate the ability to sequence events chronologically; to retain and retrieve information; to express that information in language; to recognize narrative elements such as characters, actions, and settings; and to tell a story. While elements such as themes and styles are more applicable to written language, oral narratives are valid (and predate written narratives historically) for assessing the aforementioned abilities. If a student has difficulties or irregularities specifically with forming sentences (C), rather than with either oral or written expression, this is equally likely to show up in spoken or written language when sentence formation is tested.

125. B: Students tend to remember vocabulary words when they have some kind of visual to associate with what the word means. Many students that struggle with vocabulary words often need a lot of practice in understanding these new words, so giving them multiple methods to learn the words is beneficial. Simply telling the students what words to memorize often does not work with students with disabilities that struggle with vocabulary. Answer A is incorrect because providing a multisensory model may be helpful for some students but this is more of a strategy that is used for reading fluency. Answer C is incorrect because additional vocabulary quizzes might become too overwhelming for some students. Answer D is incorrect because although a dictionary can help learn the term at first, this strategy will not likely be effective in the long term.

126. A: Giving a student like Shamus a story starter and counting his correct writing sequences is one of the most beneficial curriculum-based assessments. This assessment focuses on many areas including spelling, punctuation, and content of the writing. Students that struggle with writing will often need practice writing short stories such as these, and it is easy to monitor their progress. Answer b is incorrect because simply giving him a list of spelling words only allows the teacher to focus on one area, spelling. Answer c is incorrect because curriculum-based assessments are not designed to take an entire class period. Answer d is incorrect because giving him a picture to write about might be more appropriate for a younger student.

127. A: Although all of these strategies can be beneficial in overcoming cultural biases, learning why the bias occurs is likely to be the most effective. If teachers are able to analyze and understand why some of the biases occur, they may be able to eliminate them or overcome them. Cultural biases occur for many reasons, but it is important to understand the impact that a teacher has and what the needs of the student might be. Answer B is incorrect because being objective may not be quite as effective as showing empathy for certain students. Answer C is incorrect because not all students will likely learn the same way so they should not necessarily be treated the same. Answer D is incorrect because simply encouraging these cross-group interactions may or may not help in overcoming personal biases.

128. B: The purpose of the LRE is to ensure that students who receive special education services are in the general education setting as often as possible while still receiving the support they need. Answer A is incorrect because a student with a disability in reading fluency will need individualized instruction in that area. Answer C is incorrect because students with learning disabilities typically spend most of the day in the general education setting so they have access to their peers. Answer D is incorrect because special education classes all day would provide a restrictive environment.

129. A: In order for students to be able to generalize a skill or concept, it is important for them to practice it across various settings. Practicing name writing inside the same classroom where it was taught does not generalize this skill. It is also important to not only practice in different settings but also with assistance from a variety of people. Answer B is incorrect because practicing at home with their parents can be an effective way to generalize this skill. Answer C is incorrect because practicing in art class gives them a new environment in which to work on the same skills. Answer D is incorrect because practicing with friends can also be beneficial in generalizing the skill.

130. C: Students who receive services in the multiple disabilities category cannot be eligible in just one disability category. These students have more than one disability that impacts them to the point that one category does not meet their needs. According to IDEA, the combination of disabilities makes it so severe that they cannot be accommodated in one category. Answer A is incorrect because deaf-blindness has its own disability category. Answer B is incorrect because a student with an orthopedic impairment can be eligible for the multiple disabilities category if they are impacted by another disability as well. Answer D is incorrect because the impact of disabilities may change, and students can go from being identified as a student with multiple disabilities to a single disability over time.